MODERN WORLD NATIONS

AFGHANISTAN

AUSTRIA

BAHRAIN

BERMUDA

CHINA

CUBA

EGYPT

ETHIOPIA

REPUBLIC OF GEORGIA

GERMANY

KUWAIT

IRAN

IRAQ

ISRAEL

MEXICO

NEW ZEALAND

PAKISTAN

RUSSIA

SAUDI ARABIA

SCOTLAND

SOUTH KOREA

UKRAINE

Ukraine

Catherine W. Cooper

Series Consulting Editor
Charles F. Gritzner
South Dakota State University

CHELSEA HOUSE
PUBLISHERS
A Haights Cross Communications ◆ Company
Philadelphia

Frontispiece: Flag of Ukraine

Cover: Church constructed of wood in the Carpathian Mountains, Ukraine.

CHELSEA HOUSE PUBLISHERS

EDITOR IN CHIEF Sally Cheney
DIRECTOR OF PRODUCTION Kim Shinners
CREATIVE MANAGER Takeshi Takahashi
MANUFACTURING MANAGER Diann Grasse

Staff for UKRAINE

EDITOR Lee Marcott
PRODUCTION ASSISTANT Jaimie Winkler
PICTURE RESEARCHER Pat Holl
COVER AND SERIES DESIGNER Takeshi Takahashi
LAYOUT 21st Century Publishing and Communications, Inc.

A Haights Cross Communications ⬧ Company

http://www.chelseahouse.com

First Printing

1 3 5 7 9 8 6 4 2

Library of Congress Cataloging-in-Publication Data

Cooper, Catherine W.
   Ukraine / Catherine W. Cooper ; editor Charles F. Gritzner.
      p. cm. — (Modern world nations)
Includes bibliographical references and index.
   ISBN 0-7910-6783-1
   1. Ukraine—Juvenile literature. I. Gritzner, Charles F. II. Title. III. Series.
DK508.515 .C66 2002
947.7—dc21

                                                   2002007154

Table of Contents

1   Introducing Ukraine:
Borderland or Heartland?   9

2   Ukraine's Location and
Natural Landscape   15

3   Ukraine Through Time   29

4   Ukrainians and Their Culture   47

5   The Government of Ukraine   59

6   How Ukrainians Make a Living   69

7   Living in Ukraine Today   87

8   Outlook for the Future   103

Facts at a Glance   108
History at a Glance   110
Glossary   112
Further Reading   114
Index   115

Ukraine

The climate along the coastline of Ukraine is influenced by winds blowing from the Black Sea. As a result, the coastal region is cooler in the summer and warmer in the winter, when compared with the country's inland areas.

Introducing Ukraine: Borderland or Heartland?

A s Europe's second largest country (after Russia), Ukraine occupies the center of the continent. The country lies midway between the Atlantic Ocean on the west and Russia's Ural Mountains on the east. Romania, Moldova, Hungary, Slovakia, and Poland are on its western border; Belarus and Russia are to its north; Russia is also its neighbor on the east. The country lies north of the Sea of Azov and the Black Sea.

As a result of this "crossroads" location, Ukraine has been influenced through time by many cultures. From the south came the Greeks and Ottoman Turks, who were busily trading and colonizing across the Black Sea; from the west came various European influences, including those from Poland, Lithuania, and Scandinavia; and from the north and east, Russia cast its long and often ominous shadow. The country's architecture, spoken languages, and the ways of making a living are just some of the culture traits that have been introduced by outside peoples.

A study of the geography of Ukraine reveals how its natural landscape has also influenced its history. Physical features such as its rich soils and mineral resources have played a major role in Ukraine's economic development. Different landscapes also have attracted different people and cultures that, in turn, have influenced the country's cultural and political landscapes. These elements of unity and diversity, of stability and challenge, will guide the way to what lies ahead for this nation of approximately 50 million people in a rich, yet vulnerable part of today's world.

Is Ukraine a borderland or heartland? While the word "Ukraine" in fact means "borderland," the country has, during the course of its history, been both on the fringe and in the heart of regional political and cultural activity. After the middle of the 14th century, others controlled the region of east Europe known as Ukraine in whole or in part. Yet, in declaring its independence from the Soviet Union in 1991, Ukraine set a course for statehood for which there was little precedence. The country always has had a strong regional identity and, from time to time, fierce independence movements have arisen.

As a part of the extensive Grand Principality of Lithuania in the 14th century, then of Poland, the Russian Empire, and the Soviet Union, Ukraine was indeed a borderland, or an outlying region. From time to time, however, the people of much of present-day Ukraine existed under a common government. Ukraine's early history is marked by periods of cohesion—under the Scythians in the 9th–11th centuries and under Cossack horsemen-warriors in later centuries. All of these groups left their imprint on the landscape and culture of Ukraine

The country's national borders are now established and respected by agreements with neighboring countries. Building a viable nation, however, requires many other elements. Establishing a healthy economy and stable political institutions

A vendor offers chanterelle mushrooms for sale in downtown Kiev. Health authorities have warned Ukrainians not to buy mushrooms and berries from such vendors because they may have been grown in soil contaminated by the 1986 Chernobyl nuclear disaster.

presents major challenges to Ukrainians today.

The country and its people suffered greatly in the two World Wars of the 20th century, and during the period of Soviet control. The legacy of Soviet-controlled industry includes outdated power plants that continue to pollute the air and create other environmental problems. The resulting radioactive fallout from the disastrous 1986 nuclear accident at a power plant in the Ukrainian town of Chernobyl still pollutes waterways and the soil. This affects human health, since cows that eat grass grown on contaminated soil may produce milk that can make the people who drink it sick. As Ukraine builds

The natural landscape features in the region extend across country borders providing both links and barriers between Ukraine and its neighboring contries. Ukraine has a long border with Russia and along the coastline of the Black Sea.

a modern industry and economy, its people are also addressing these environmental issues.

Fortunately, the soil found throughout much of Ukraine is among the world's most fertile types. Thus Ukraine has long been known for the rich abundance and variety of its agricultural products. Under natural, uncultivated conditions, the vast plains and gently rolling hills have a natural cover of grasses. The *steppes* (drier areas covered with short grasses), prairies (covered with taller grasses common to areas with more abundant precipitation), and forested areas of the country have natural beauty. People enjoy hiking and skiing on the mountain trails, and sunbathing and swimming at Black Sea beaches.

Since declaring independence from the Soviet Union in 1991, Ukrainians have worked to establish a feeling of unity and "nationhood." One of the first concerns has been distinguishing its language from that of Russia's. The Ukrainian form of Cyrillic writing style somewhat differs from the Russian form, and employs a slightly different alphabet. This is reflected in the translation of words into other languages, such as English. For example, when the Ukrainian alphabet is used as the basis for spelling an English word, the spelling is different than when the English word is based on the Russian alphabet. Currently, the most common and familiar spellings used for Ukrainian place names are based on the Russian alphabet ("Kiev," for example). But as Ukrainian-based writing becomes more widely recognized, some of the place names will be written differently in English; these "new" spellings (such as "Kyiv" for "Kiev") are given in parentheses in this book.

Ukraine is a beautiful place with rich natural resources, a long history of seeking unity and independence, and an opportunity now to build a solid nation. Understanding the country's physical and human geography is an important step toward gaining an appreciation of its people, the pride they have in their land, and the challenges they face today.

Much of Ukraine is quite flat, but its Carpathian Mountains are similar in height to the Appalachian Mountains in the United States, which reach a peak elevation of 6,684 feet.

2

Ukraine's Location and Natural Landscape

U kraine's physical geography—its natural landscape—is a very important element in helping shape the country's history, its culture, and its current condition. The competing themes of "borderland" and "heartland" have characterized the country's history for centuries.

Location

Ukraine is one of the westernmost countries to emerge from the Union of Soviet Socialist Republics (USSR). It has a long border with Russia and along the coastline of the Black Sea.

In absolute location, Ukraine extends as far north as approximately 52° 20' north latitude and as far south as 44° 29' north, at Yalta on the south coast of the Crimean Peninsula. Its farthest western extent is adjacent to Slovakia at about 22° 18' east longitude. In the east, it extends to approximately 42° east longitude.

Ukraine is one of Europe's newest countries and also one of its largest. When it broke from the Soviet Union in 1991, it retained the borders it had as a republic of the USSR. As an independent country, it is second only to Russia in size among the European nations. Ukraine has an area of 233,090 square miles (603,700 square kilometers). This is about the size of Arizona and New Mexico combined, or a little smaller than Texas.

The capital city, Kiev (Kyiv), is also the country's largest, and is located in the north-central part of the country, at 50° 27' north latitude. This places the city farther north than any part of the United States except Alaska, and at approximately the same parallel as the Canadian city of Winnipeg, Manitoba (49° 53' north latitude). At this latitude, Kiev's winter days are short. In midwinter, around December 21, the sun rises at approximately 8:00 A.M. and sets at approximately 4:00 P.M. giving only about eight hours of sunlight. In late June, on the other hand, Kiev's residents enjoy approximately 16 hours of sunlight.

The entire area of Ukraine falls in the same time zone, which is two hours ahead of Greenwich Mean Time (GMT). So, when it is noon in Greenwich (London), England, it is 2:00 P.M. in Ukraine. This difference in time zones illustrates an important relationship between time and longitude. The earth is 360° in circumference. It rotates once every 24 hours, so each hour corresponds to a difference in longitude of 15° (360°/24 hours = 15°/1 hour). Thus, Philadelphia, Pennsylvania, at 75° west longitude, is five hours *behind* GMT (0° longitude) and seven hours behind Kiev time (30° east longitude). When it is 2:00 P.M. in Kiev and noon in London, it is 7:00 A.M. in Philadelphia.

Natural Landscape

Physical geography has played a vital role in the culture (way of life) and the history of the region through the ages. For instance, in the fifth century B.C., the grasslands of the east allowed horsemen to cross easily into the region. In the late 1940s, Ukrainians used its mountainous region for protection as they resisted the Soviet military.

Natural Vegetation. The grasslands of Ukraine and western Russia are steppes (pronounced "steps"). The natural vegetation is relatively short grass, or a mixture of grass and shrubs. In this semiarid region the grasses are shorter and less dense than those on prairie land. Toward the north and west, the short grasslands give way to the taller grasses of prairies. Both the steppes and prairies are located on flat to gently rolling plains.

The rich steppe soil supports wildflowers in abundance, poppies, sunflowers, daisies, lilacs, and others. Flowers are cultivated for nectar and for honey production.

In the northern and western regions of the country, the prairie gives way to mixed broadleaf forests, with trees such as oak, elm, beech, and maple, as well as coniferous forests of pine. Over one-third of Ukraine's original forests have been cleared for agricultural production. Currently, the forest-prairie region covers approximately one-third of the country.

Water Features. Ukraine has approximately 3,000 rivers, many flowing southward across the country to the Black Sea. For thousands of years, the rivers have brought silt from upstream and deposited it when the streams reached the flat lowlands. These deposits of alluvium (water-deposited silt), in combination with rich grassland sod, have created some of the most fertile soils in the world. In addition, the waterways made easy transportation corridors from the Baltic Sea to the Black Sea. This route attracted the Vikings from the north to Ukraine, where they settled in the ninth century A.D. The story of these Vikings, what brought them to the region, and what became of them is told in the next chapter.

The Dnieper (Dnipro) River flows southward from Russia through Belarus and enters Ukraine near Chernobyl (Chornobyl). Over the centuries, the Dnieper River has been the central traffic corridor through the heart of the Ukrainian

The Dnieper River, shown here as it flows through Kiev, has been the major transportation corridor through the heart of Ukraine for centuries.

region. It also has been the dividing line often used to partition Ukraine among the spheres of influence of neighboring states. So the Dnieper has been crucial to defining Ukraine as heartland or borderland, core or periphery.

Kiev is on the Dnieper. Below Kiev, the river flows southeast, makes a turn of about 90 degrees to flow southwest, and empties into the Black Sea. Three huge dams have altered the Dnieper's natural flow and formed reservoirs in Ukraine; they contain power plants that provide hydroelectric energy. Ukraine's second most important river, the Dniester (Dnister), is located in the far southwestern corner of the country. It flows from headwaters rising in the nearby Carpathian Mountains, and forms part of the country's border with Moldova.

The coastal waters of the Black Sea and the Sea of Azov form Ukraine's southern border. This border is approximately 1,800 miles (2,900 kilometers) long and includes the coast of Crimea, a peninsula that extends into the Black Sea. An arm of the Black Sea reaches through the Kerch Strait, a narrow water passage separating Ukraine and Russia, and forms the Sea of Azov.

The Black Sea has had a profound influence on Ukrainian history, economy, and culture. It is both a barrier separating neighbors and a highway facilitating trade and communication. The early people who put to sea on its waters were intimidated by its sudden violent storms. This may be the reason the Turks called it the "Black" Sea.

The Black Sea and the Sea of Azov have a water surface of 178,000 square miles (164,000 square kilometers). The maximum depth of the Black Sea is over 7,250 feet (2,210 meters). Because of the many rivers bringing fresh water to it, the sea's salinity (salt content) is only about half that of the ocean.

Another unusual natural feature of the Black Sea is its "dead zone," which lies about 250 feet (76 meters) below the

The culture of Ukraine has been shaped by it neighbors around the Black Sea.

surface. Above the dead zone is an upper layer rich with sturgeon, mackerel, anchovy, and other varieties of sea life. In the dead zone below, however, there is no dissolved oxygen and marine life is unable to live. This dead zone is attributed to a high level of hydrogen sulfide, but the cause or origin of which is not known.

Unfortunately, since the late 20th century, the rich upper layer of the Black Sea has also become depleted. Human-caused pollution is taking a heavy toll on the once abundant aquatic populations. Human and industrial wastes, as well as agricultural chemicals—applied to the cropland and washed into waterways—pollute the rivers that flow to the Black Sea. The Black Sea also contributes to the climate of coastal Ukraine. The nearby land is influenced by winds blowing from the sea; compared with the country's inland areas, the coastal region is cooler in summer and warmer in winter. The coastal area is also more humid than the drier inland regions due to the moisture carried from the sea.

Along the southwestern edge of Ukraine's Black Sea coastline lies the large port city of Odessa (Odesa). Farther west and south along the coast, near Ukraine's border with Romania, is a segment of the Danube River delta. (The majority of the delta lies in Romania). This important river makes a 1,776-mile (2,860-kilometer) journey across central and Eastern Europe from its headwaters in the mountains of Germany, culminating at the Black Sea, where its delta forms an extensive low, wetland marsh area.

There are other vast areas of wetlands in the country. Particularly notable are those located along much of the course of the Dnieper River and the famous Pripet Marshes in the north. This huge wetland is Europe's largest marsh; it extends across Ukraine's northern border into neighboring Belarus. Portions of the Pripet Marshes have been drained and cleared.

Landforms. Ukraine has relatively little physical relief. Much of the country is quite flat; the average elevation is only 574 feet (175 meters) above sea level, about the same elevation as the highest point in Louisiana. Only in the western part of Ukraine does the elevation rise. South and west of Kiev is an uplands area broken by river valleys, some with canyons as deep as 1,000 feet (305 meters). Only 5 percent of the country is mountainous: the Crimean Mountains located on the peninsula of the same name, and a short stretch of the Carpathian Mountains in the southwest. The Carpathians form an arc through the Czech Republic, northern Slovakia, southern Poland, Ukraine, and Romania. The highest point in Ukraine is Mount Hoverla, which rises to 6,762 feet (2,061 meters) in the Carpathians. In contrast, the highest peak in the Appalachian Mountains of the eastern United States is North Carolina's Mt. Mitchell at 6,684 feet (2,037 meters).

The Crimean Mountains, which rise to over 5,000 feet (1,524 meters), are separated from the coast by a strip of land typically five to eight miles wide (8–13 kilometers). The town of Yalta, the port of Sevastopol, and a series of resort communities are located on this coast.

Climate

The climate of Ukraine is generally midlatitude temperate continental, but several different zones are apparent. Northern and northwestern Ukraine experience a humid continental climate with cool summers and rather long, harsh winters. Winter temperatures in December, January, and February are usually below freezing but seldom drop below 14° F (–10° C). Summer temperatures, in June, July, and August, are in the range of 60° to 80°F (16° to 27°C). The climate of northern Ukraine is milder than might be expected considering its high latitude. The moderating winds bring warmer air from the distant Atlantic Ocean, since there are no major north-south trending mountains to block them.

The southern half of the country has a dry continental, or midlatitude steppe, climate, which is drier and experiences occasional drought. Heaviest rainfall occurs during the summer months, often falling in heavy thundershowers accompanied by lightning and thunder. The Crimean Peninsula is dry with hot summers and mild winters. Much of it gets less than 16 inches (41 centimeters) of precipitation annually.

Along the south coast of Crimea is a band of Mediterranean climate, the same climate type that allows the cultivation of citrus fruits, grapes, vegetables, and other subtropical crops in coastal California and of olives and grapes in Italy, Greece, and some other lands immediately adjacent to the Mediterranean Sea.

Precipitation varies across the country. The Carpathian Mountain region receives the most rainfall, with an average of 50 inches (127 centimeters) per year. The annual rainfall around Kiev averages 24 inches (61 centimeters). (Similar amounts of precipitation occur throughout much of the interior plains of the United States, extending from the Dakotas to central Texas.) Apart from the mountainous area, the southern part of Ukraine receives less precipitation than the northern area.

The following table gives the temperature and precipitation patterns for Kiev and for Simperopol in Crimea and points up the differences in the two parts of the country. The northern city of Kiev, when compared with Simperopol in the south, shows more precipitation and lower temperatures on average.

Comparative Climate Data–Kiev and Simperopol

AVERAGE DAILY TEMPERATURE

	Kiev HIGH	Kiev LOW	Simperopol HIGH	Simperopol LOW
January	24°F (-4°C)	14°F (-10°C)	37°F (3°C)	24°F (-5°C)
February	28°F (-2°C)	17°F (-8°C)	40°F (5°C)	26°F (-3°C)
March	37°F (3°C)	25°F (-4°C)	47°F (9°C)	31°F (-1°C)
April	56°F (14°C)	41°F (5°C)	60°F (16°C)	41°F (5°C)
May	69°F (21°C)	51°F (11°C)	71°F (22°C)	50°F (10°C)
June	75°F (24°C)	56°F (14°C)	78°F (25°C)	57°F (14°C)
July	77°F (25°C)	59°F (15°C)	82°F (28°C)	60°F (16°C)
August	76°F (24°C)	58°F (14°C)	82°F (28°C)	60°F (15°C)
September	68°F (20°C)	50°F (10°C)	74°F (23°C)	53°F (12°C)
October	56°F (13°C)	42°F (6°C)	63°F (17°C)	44°F (7°C)
November	42°F (6°C)	32°F (0°C)	54°F (12°C)	40°F (4°C)
December	30°F (-1°C)	22°F (-6°C)	44°F (7°C)	32°F (0°C)

AVERAGE MONTHLY PRECIPITATION

	Kiev	Simperopol
January	2.3 inches (58 mm)	1.8 inches (46 mm)
February	2.3 inches (59 mm)	1.5 inches (37 mm)
March	2.0 inches (51 mm)	1.6 inches (40 mm)
April	1.8 inches (45 mm)	1.1 inches (28 mm)
May	1.9 inches (49 mm)	1.5 inches (38 mm)
June	2.2 inches (55 mm)	1.4 inches (35 mm)
July	3.6 inches (91 mm)	2.5 inches (64 mm)
August	3.6 inches (91 mm)	1.5 inches (39 mm)
September	1.2 inches (30 mm)	1.4 inches (36 mm)
October	1.3 inches (33 mm)	0.9 inches (24mm)
November	2.2 inches (56 mm)	1.7 inches (43 mm)
December	2.3 inches (59 mm)	2.1 inches (52 mm)
TOTAL ANNUAL	26.7 inches (677 mm)	19 inches (482 mm)

Source: United States National Climate Center: *Climate Normals for the United States (Base 1951-80)*

Much of Ukraine has a rich, black soil that has allowed agriculture to be a basic economic livelihood for the region for many centuries.

Soil

As has already been mentioned, Ukraine is blessed with some of the world's most fertile soils—rich, black "Chernozems." This thick soil, noted for its high content of humus (organic material), occupies almost two-thirds of the country. It is the foundation of Ukraine's reputation as the "breadbasket of Europe." Agriculture has been a basic economic livelihood of Ukrainians for many centuries.

Chernozem soils are a type of "mollisol," which underlies the world's great steppe and prairie regions. In addition to the steppes of Ukraine and Russia, other areas of mollisols include the prairies of North America and the pampas of Argentina. Mollisols are soft, even when they are dry, and they are crumbly to touch. The have a high content of humus, or organic matter, some of which comes from the roots of the surface grasses as they continually decay and renew themselves. The grasses have large root systems that decay quickly compared with woody matter. This is because the organic matter from grass roots does not have to work its way down into the soil from the surface as do decaying leaves and tree branches. The resulting humus gives the soil its dark color and is the primary factor contributing to its high fertility.

Dry lands such as those in Ukraine typically burn periodically in short rotational periods. This fire is an important element in creating natural vegetation communities. It causes the release of minerals, such as calcium, magnesium, sodium, and potassium, that plants need in order to grow. Fire also tends to kill woody vegetation, including many varieties of trees, resulting in grasses that thrive in the more open, shadeless, environment. Many scientists believe that early people, using fire as a hunting tool, were responsible for creating steppe and prairie grasslands including those extending across much of Ukraine and beyond.

This combination of natural features—flat land, adequate moisture, and extremely fertile soil—created an environment ideal for the growing of wheat. Over the centuries, several varieties of this important grain were developed in Ukraine. When many Ukrainians settled in North America during the 1800s, they found that their own seed varieties were much better adapted to the prairies than were the varieties of wheat that had come from England and other wetter areas of western Europe.

Other Natural Resources

Beneath the earth's surface in Ukraine are substantial deposits of natural resources. Rich deposits of coal and iron ore are located in the far eastern part of the country. The Donets

Ukraine has relatively little relief. Much of the country is quite flat with an average elevation of only 574 feet (175 meters). Its great number of rivers (nearly 3,000) and the proximity to both the Black Sea and the Sea of Azov have had a profound influence on Ukraine's livelihood and commerce.

(Donbas; Donets'k) Basin is world-famous for its extensive deposits of high quality coal. Deposits of iron ore abound in the region of Krivoy Rog (Kryvy Rih). Rail connections over the approximately 250 miles between these two areas have helped make them major industrial centers. Ukraine also has uranium, natural gas, and oil resources. Other mineral deposits include manganese, titanium, bauxite, and salt.

National Parks and Natural Reserves

Ukraine has several large natural reserves. Askaniya-Nova, located in the steppe region, was designated a private reserve in 1875 and became a national park in 1919. (In 1872, Yellowstone was established as the first national park in the United States.) Askaniya-Nova became an approved Biosphere Reserve under a UNESCO program in 1985.

Two other units have been accepted as Biosphere Reserves—Chernomorskiy (also called the Black Sea Nature Reserve) and Carpathian. The Black Sea Nature Reserve was established in 1927 and includes some portions of the sea itself, protecting the waterfowl that congregate there. The Carpathian Biosphere Reserve protects a beech forest that has never been cut for timber. It is the only such forest left in Europe. The Shasky National Park in the far northwestern part of the country protects a wooded lake district. The Danube Water Meadows protects the region in Ukraine near the mouth of the Danube River.

In its various parts, Ukraine is home to wolves, fox, lynx, martens, deer, and other mammals. The Carpathian wildcat is legally protected. The Crimean Mountains are home to wild pigs and mountain sheep.

The country has over 350 species of birds. (North America has about 800 species.) Birds of the steppes include buzzards, unusual falcons, and harriers, as well as Demoiselle cranes and the Steppe eagle. The Danube delta area is a rich wetland and home to several species of pelicans. Because the Sea of Azov is shallow and its coast has many inlets, it is attractive to herons, egrets, and other wading birds.

The features of the Ukrainian landscape and the country's natural resources have attracted peoples through the ages. Much of Ukraine's history is thus the story of how these people have moved across the region and how and where they have settled.

This tapestry of a Scythian horseman dates from the 5th century B.C. This culture of fierce warriors flourished from the 7th to the 4th centuries B.C. in the steppes north of the Black Sea.

Ukraine Through Time

Dominated by different neighbors from time to time through the ages, different parts of Ukraine had different cultural and political experiences. One of the keys to understanding the country today is to study the historic experiences of the different regions. For instance, communities bordering the Black Sea had commercial connections with traders to the south and with the maritime powers of the Mediterranean Sea. The northern and western forest/steppe region was tied by waterways to Europe and had settled agricultural communities. The eastern and central steppe region saw waves of horsemen thunder in from the east.

Early People

Groups of nomadic people inhabited the area that is now Ukraine as early as 5000 B.C. The first of these was the Trypillians, who raised wheat and other grains as well as sheep, cattle, and horses. Prominent among the peoples that followed were the nomadic Scythians, who flourished on the steppes north of the Black Sea from the seventh to the fourth centuries B.C. The Scythians were fierce warriors and superb horsemen who actively traded with Greek outposts in the region. The Scythians supplied the Greeks with honey, grain, furs, cattle, and slaves, and received in return wine, textiles, weapons, and art. The finely crafted gold work that has been found in Scythian tombs is of Greek origin and attests to the early trade. Scythian burial mounds have been found on the steppes.

Why the Scythians declined in population and importance, and what eventually happened to these hardy horsemen of the plains, is unknown. Perhaps an extended drought depleted their food supply. But, as the Scythians declined in Ukraine, another nomadic people replaced them.

Early in the Christian era (the period following the birth of Christ), Ostrogoths, a Germanic people, controlled most of Ukraine. They, in turn, were subjugated by the Huns, fierce warriors who exploded out of their Siberian homeland to spread throughout much of Eastern Europe. Slavic peoples from the northern Carpathian Mountains spread across the Ukraine in the sixth and seventh centuries A.D. These Slavs spread their culture slowly and peacefully over a wide area. Over time, their language lost its consistency and evolved into three subgroups. One of the language groups was East Slavic, parent language of today's Ukrainian, Russian, and Belorussian tongues.

According to legend, Kiev was founded during the Slavic expansion in the seventh century. A tribal leader name Kyi (Ky) and his two brothers and a sister picked the site on the bluffs above the Dnieper River, on the west bank (the right bank as one faces downstream). They believed the location was an ideal site for developing a regional trading center. Because of its location on a bluff overlooking the river, it also could be easily defended.

A different cultural element was introduced into southeastern Ukraine with the arrival of the Khazars, who were Turkic and Iranian people from the Caucasus region located to the east, between the Black and Caspian seas. The Khazars eventually settled in the region during the eighth century, establishing their capital and major trading center near the mouth of the Volga River at Itil. This location, where the Volga flows into the Caspian Sea, was important; not only were the Khazars able to conduct a lively trade with the neighboring Slavic people, but they went on to build a huge commercial empire. By settling north of the Caucasus Mountains, the Khazars also effectively blocked Arabs from invading northward and westward into Ukraine and farther into Europe.

By the second half of the eighth century, the Khazars had expanded westward and controlled Ukraine to the Dnieper River. They built towns, engaged in farming, and were actively involved in trade and commerce. In an unusual occurrence, the ruling class of Khazars adopted Judaism in about 740. Rarely has conversion to Judaism happened en masse, and why this happened with the Khazars is not known. While some of the original Khazar settlers were Jewish, the mass conversion was most likely instigated by a headman proclaiming it should be done.

Kievan Rus

During the eighth and ninth centuries, Scandinavians ventured far from their northern home, spreading west, east, and south—eventually as far as the region now known as Ukraine. Some raided, and settled in, England, Ireland, and France, while others sailed further west to colonize Iceland. These Vikings eventually also traveled across the Atlantic Ocean, settling in Greenland and even reaching—temporarily—North America. Other Norsemen known as Varangians, probably from Sweden, crossed the Baltic Sea and established settlements in what is now Estonia and Latvia. From these small countries facing the Baltic, they continued southward, establishing a fortress and trading center at Novgorod, which is in present-day Russia.

Over time they found the waterways, including the mighty Volga River, that linked the Baltic with the Caspian Sea. Once they found and were able to control this vital route, they established strong commercial links with the Islamic world. The Varangians also found river links to the Dnieper River and on to the Black Sea. This step ultimately led them to the region's most important trading city at the time—Constantinople, capital of Byzantium (present-day Istanbul, Turkey).

In 862, a Scandinavian named Oleg won control of Kiev and established the state of Kievan (Kyivan) Rus. Ukraine, Russia, and Belarus all trace their national history to this Eastern Slavic state. Oleg made Kiev his capital and the center of his trading realm, making this a period when Ukraine was indeed a "heartland," or an important "core" region. Kievan Rus traders moved along the Dnieper River and along connecting portages south to Byzantium and north to the Baltic. It was a "water road," a "road from the Varangians to the Greeks." In 965, the Kievan warrior-prince Sviatoslav took his forces into the Khazars' territory, crushed their armies, and destroyed their capital, Itil. Thereafter, the Khazars' influence north of the Black Sea declined, and Kievan Rus dominated trade, for a time, on the Volga route. Under a series of strong rulers, Kievan Rus developed trade and commerce, extracted tribute, and influenced a vast territory for the next 350 years.

Valdimir the Great (980–1015) acquired new territories, Galicia and Volhynia (Volyn), for Kievan Rus. These were princedoms west and southwest of Kiev, including stretches of the Carpathian Mountains. These lands changed hands between Ukraine and its neighbors a number of times in the years to come. Valdimir the Great established settlements south of Kiev to protect the people against invaders. Kievan Rus thus became the largest state in Europe, although at that time "states," or countries, were a loose collection of principalities rather than the cohesive states of today with clearly defined borders and centralized political institutions.

To help unify the people of Kievan Rus, Validmir looked for a religion to replace the people's pagan practices. He converted to Byzantine Christianity in 988 and had most of the people of Kiev baptized en masse in the Dnieper River as the first step to having all his subjects convert. With the religious conversion came greater communication with European royalty, as well as expansion of the arts, monastic learning, innovative architecture, and even a basic structured legal system. Two Greek missionaries composed a writing system for the Ukrainian language using a Cyrillian style of writing. Classes of craftsmen, clergy, and merchants developed. Construction of St. Sophia Cathedral in Kiev, modeled on Hagia Sophia in Constantinople, was begun in 1017. This structure serves as an illustration of the dramatic change in culture in Ukraine during this period.

Sons of rulers contested who would be the next ruler of Kievan Rus, and the conflicts weakened the controlling government. In the late 11th century, the trade route through Kiev declined in importance as a result of two major factors: first, north-south trade between the Baltic and Black sea regions had become less important; and second, trade between Europe and places to the east relied increasingly on Mediterranean Sea trading centers. New raiders from Asia also began to challenge the Kievan Rus. Mongols under Batu Khan, grandson of Genghis Khan, conquered Kiev in 1240, marking the end of the Kievan Rus period of Ukrainian history.

The Golden Horde

Although Kievan Rus never covered all of present-day Ukraine, it exercised more centralized control than had the various bands that previously had lived in the region. With the

A Persian painting from the 15th century A.D. depicts the Mongol warriors who had swept westward across the continent as far as Central Europe, but by that century the Mongols had begun to be pushed back.

mid-13th-century conquest by the Mongols, or the "Golden Horde," the large and somewhat cohesive area and peoples of Ukraine began to be pulled in different directions. The region became more like a border to other neighboring lands rather than a distinct central core of culture and power. The "borderland" period of Ukraine's history had begun.

Again, different parts of the Ukraine had different experiences:

- The two principalities of Galicia and Volhynia, in the southwestern region extending along the Dniester River to the Black Sea, retained their Kievan Rus heritage for a time.

- In Crimea, the Muslims established a "Khanate" and became vassals of the Ottoman Turk Empire based in Constantinople. The people of the Crimean Khanate were called Tatars.

- The Golden Horde held sway over much of the central part of the region.

Ukraine's European neighbor to the northwest, the Grand Principality of Lithuania, grew strong, and Lithuanian princes gradually moved eastward, pushing back the Golden Horde. The people of Ukraine generally welcomed them and were incorporated into local government. Lithuanian newcomers adopted the local culture, accepting the Orthodox Christian religion and the local language throughout the 14th and early 15th centuries. But gradually, the Lithuanian influence gave way to Polish dominance in neighboring Ukrainian lands.

Galicia and Volhynia had come under the dominance of Poland. In the mid-14th century, a Polish king had set out to control the region, justifying the action, in part, as an effort to extend the Roman Catholic faith over people practicing Orthodoxy. Increasingly, Polish influence made a strong imprint on the people of the region—most became Roman Catholic; Latin became the official language, and the head of the government was Polish. Members of Ukraine's elite popu-lation became less interested in local affairs as they identified increasingly with the ruling culture. In the late 16th century, a particularly Ukrainian faith was formed, the Uniate Church. It acknowledged the Pope in Rome as leader, but retained Orthodox forms of worship. The new faith reflected the history and different influences at play in the region.

The Cossacks

As Polish institutions, such as Roman Catholicism and serfdom, became more dominant in the west, many Ukrainians in opposition looked to the sparsely inhabited eastern steppe region called the "wild fields" as a place to settle. For centuries, people had traveled there seasonally to hunt, fish, and gather honey. Now people from Polish-controlled areas in the west began to move eastward to escape the life of the serfs, who were virtually slaves to the owner of the land on which they lived.

These "refugees" from the west joined bands of horsemen called Cossacks. The word comes from "kazak," which is from a Turkic language and means "adventurer" or "freeman." Cossacks trace their name and history from the 11th century to the Tatar groups north of the Caspian Sea. As peasants also fled Poland and Lithuania to escape serfdom, they were incorporated into Cossack bands. By the mid-16th century, a large community of Cossacks had developed. These people practiced a rudimentary form of democracy—they elected their leader, called a "hetman," and many decisions were made through a representative group.

Both Poland and Russia recognized the warrior skill of the Cossacks and engaged them to fight people beyond their borders. Although these two countries tried to control them, the proud Cossacks kept their independence. They fought Turks to the south and east and also provided a buffer protecting Poland against the Tatars (even though they refused to come under Polish domination). In the wars and related violence, many Ukrainian soldiers died; so too, however, did many clergy, Jews, and Polish landlords and officials. In 1649, the hetman Bohdan Khmelnytsky defeated the Polish armies and arrived in Kiev as a liberator. Polish opposition continued, however, as Khmelnytsky tried to create a Cossack state focused on the steppes east of the Dnieper River. He sought help from the Russian tsar (pronounced "zar"), which was confirmed in 1654 by the Pereyaslav agreement. Although Khmelnytsky sought only foreign aid, Russia used this treaty to begin its long period of increasing control over Ukraine.

The following years were unsettled ones as rival Cossacks bid for power and Russia and Poland vied for influence. A formal partition of Ukraine between Poland and Muscovy (Russia) occurred in 1667 with the Treaty of Ardrusovo. After that, Poland and Lithuania continued their dominance west of the Dnieper River, increasingly drawing the people there under European influence. The local nobility identified with their peers in Europe, and the serfs continued to be exploited.

Russian influence increased in the east after 1667. In the late 1700s, the armies of Catherine the Great of Russia eliminated the Cossack military in southern Ukraine. This event dissolved the last vestige of the Hetmanate. Russia moved southward to annex Crimea in 1783. The city of Odessa was rebuilt on the Black Sea coast and grew to become an important seaport and cosmopolitan center. In a series of partitions, Poland gave up control of much of the land west of the Dnieper River to Russia. The far southwest, around Lviv, was annexed to Hapsburg Austria. Ukraine effectively had become a borderland of Russia, although it was a very important outlying region.

The Crimean War and the Late 19th Century

Western Europe focused its attention on Ukraine in 1854 when the Crimean War broke out. The basic conflict was between Moscow and the Turks over who would speak for the Christians in the Muslim Ottoman Empire, which included much of Ukraine. Great Britain and France were concerned about the spreading influence of Russia and supported the Turkish ruler (sultan) in the conflict.

In this war, British soldiers arrived in the Black Sea, but landed with inadequate supplies to lay siege to the port of Sevastopol. In the cold, rain, and mud, and with little food, many soldiers died from exposure or hunger, as well as from enemy action. The British government had learned from newspaper accounts that the wounded were in crowded hospitals without blankets, clean bedding, or food they could swallow. At the request of her government, Florence Nightingale led about 40 nurses to the area. She withstood the anger and opposition of military leaders and doctors. Eventually the nurses were allowed to cook reasonable food for the hospitalized men, clean their wounds, and supply straw mattresses and clean sheets from Nightingale's own funds. The soldiers called her the "Lady with the Lamp." Her actions and dedication gave rise to the beginning of nursing as a highly respected career.

The Crimean War was known also for inspiring the "Charge of the Light Brigade," a work by British poet Alfred, Lord Tennyson. This famous poem memorialized the brave soldiers who followed garbled orders to move against an enemy position that was so strong the Englishmen could not possibly succeed. Ultimately, however, the siege was successful and the Russians withdrew from Sevastopol. The Treaty of Paris, in 1856, ended the conflict.

Other changes were taking place in Ukraine. Serfdom ended in 1861 and laborers, freed from bondage to the land, were available for other types of work. Industrial development was encouraged, especially in the Donbas region of eastern Ukraine. A working class of people not engaged in agriculture began to emerge in this increasingly important region. The Russian rulers, called "tsars", felt the need to develop natural resources and industrialize their country, so they mined the coal and iron ore of Ukraine, and factories began appearing in Kiev and Odessa.

The tsars, however, feared the nationalist feelings of Ukrainians, and in the middle of the 19th century, while the

A nineteenth-century illustration by Robert Riggs depicts Florence Nightingale working as a nurse in the Crimean War; she served at the request of the British government, which was concerned about the health of its soldiers in the field.

region was under their control, they abolished the Uniate Church. Ministers of the Russian government banned Ukrainian writings at about the same time, and basic education levels declined. A few writers, such as Taras Shevchenko (1814–1861), whose work seemed to promote nationalistic feelings, were exiled.

In the southwest, in Galicia, people living under the Austrian Empire often lacked sufficient land to have farms on which they could successfully provide adequate food and other necessities. Between approximately 1880 and 1914, many of these poor, landless people left the region to seek a better life in Western Europe or North America. Those who stayed behind increasingly developed a strong consciousness of their distinctive Ukrainian heritage.

World War I and the Interwar Years

The First World War broke out in September 1914. Fierce battles between the Austro-Hungarian forces and those of Russia were fought in Ukraine. Each side accused Ukrainians of helping the enemy, resulting in their being treated very harshly by both military forces.

While World War I was being fought, another major event occurred in the region. The Russian Revolution began in 1917 with the overthrow of the Russian tsar. The revolutionary party members, called Bolsheviks, under the leadership of Lenin, took control of the government in Moscow. Initially, it appeared that Ukraine would now achieve a level of self-determination. A representative governmental body was established in Kiev, and a president was elected. In Galicia, a Western Ukrainian State was established and the two governments in the west and the east united briefly in 1919.

Ukraine, however, was a continuing stage for military action. When World War I ended in 1918, Bolshevik armies continued to fight the so-called White Russians, who supported the tsar and the former Russian Empire. The Polish army then fought the Red (Bolshevik) Army in western Ukraine. Throughout these conflicts, Ukrainian nationalists fought to gain their own independence as a country.

In 1921, the military conflicts ended. Parts of Ukraine were annexed to the Czechoslovak Republic and to Romania; Poland incorporated Galicia and several other small territories. The rest of the territory became Soviet Ukraine. In 1922, the Ukrainian Soviet Socialist Republic (SSR) was incorporated into the Communist country of the Union of Soviet Socialist Republics (USSR).

The Soviet government, centered in Moscow, now controlled the Ukrainian economy and agriculture, both of which had suffered severely during the war. As many as one million Ukrainian people died in a severe famine in 1921-22. A subsequent brief period of less stringent regulation by Moscow allowed agriculture to revive. During this period, there was an accompanying growth of Ukrainian institutions with expanded education, publication of Ukrainian books, and encouragement of national culture.

In the late 1920s, however, Joseph Stalin's economic plan for the USSR forced dramatic and harsh changes. From the central government in Moscow, the dictator ordered new mines and factories built in Ukraine. He ordered that family farms be merged into "collectives," with quotas imposed for producing certain quantities of food. Farmers became workers on the new state-owned farms; they received only food from the government in payment for their labor. Those who hesitated to turn their land, livestock, and machinery over to the government were forced to comply. If they resisted, they were killed, or deported to remote and frigid Siberia. People who worked on the collectives could not eat what they grew, but had to deliver it to government officials. These strict policies caused yet another devastating famine. It is estimated that during 1932–1933 as many as seven million people may have starved to death.

During this same period, Soviet policy toward culture in general changed. The Soviets were particularly harsh in suppressing the activities of Ukrainian Orthodox clergy, intellectuals, writers, and the cultural elite.

World War II and the Postwar Soviet Period

In 1939, German military forces launched World War II. German Nazi leader Adolf Hitler carved Galicia from Poland and incorporated it into Russian Ukraine. Then, in 1941, Hitler did the unexpected when he turned on his former ally, the Soviet Union, and invaded the huge country. The war on Germany's eastern front was fought in the USSR, much of it in

Sixty percent of Ukrainian Jews were exterminated by the Nazis during the Holocaust. Some met their end at the side of a grave that had already been prepared for them. In 1941 the Nazis ordered Jewish people of the city of Kiev to prepare for transport away from their homes. Instead, 34,000 were taken a short distance away to Babyn Yar and massacred.

Ukrainian Russia. Kiev was besieged for 80 days in 1941 and was again the scene of frantic fighting in 1943. Initially, Ukrainians welcomed the Germans, seeing them as liberators from the Soviets. But this positive perception changed quickly: the Nazis engaged in the mass killing of Jews in Ukraine and forced many people to go to Germany as slave laborers.

The Red Army counteroffensive began in 1943, and the Soviets gradually regained Ukraine. In 1944, Stalin forcefully removed the Tatars from Crimea, deporting almost 200,000 of them to Uzbekestan, declaring that they had helped the Nazis. In February 1945, the heads of state of the United States, Great Britain, and the Soviet Union met in Crimea. At this Yalta Conference, U.S. president Franklin Roosevelt, British prime minister Winston Churchill, and Joseph Stalin determined how various parts of European territory would be governed by the allies following the defeat of Nazi Germany.

At the end of the war, the borders on the western edge of Ukraine were redrawn. Poland was forced to give up Galicia and other territories. These and other lands that had been in Czechoslovakia and other neighboring countries were returned to Ukraine, and therefore to the USSR.

Ukraine suffered enormously in World War II. The fighting destroyed villages, towns and cities; industrial plants were leveled; farms, including buildings and agricultural equipment, were destroyed; and transportation facilities, including railroad tracks and trains, highways, port facilities, and airports, were ruined. It is estimated that over 700 cities and towns were destroyed in whole or in part. Over 80 percent of Kiev was destroyed. Ukraine had a population of approximately 40 million in 1940; approximately 5.3 million died in the war, and another 2.3 million were sent to Germany as slave laborers. Sixty percent of Ukraine's Jews were lost in the Holocaust. Over 40 percent of the economy was destroyed, and ten million people were left homeless.

The hardships continued after the war, as an estimated 300,000 people suspected of disloyalty to the USSR were sent to concentration camps, often in desolate Siberia. A drought was widespread in 1946, causing the people of western Ukraine to suffer a severe famine that lasted from 1946 to 1948.

Those who believed in Ukrainian independence continued fighting after World War II in western Ukraine. These "partisans" threatened Soviet troops and were not totally eliminated until the early 1950s.

Stalin died in 1953, and Nikita Khrushchev became leader of the USSR. Khrushchev had spent his early career in Ukraine. In 1954, on the occasion of the 300th anniversary of the union of Russia and Ukraine, Khrushchev transferred the Crimean Peninsula from the Russian Soviet Federated Socialist Republic to the Ukraine Soviet Socialist Republic. In this act, Khrushchev was harking back to the treaty between Russia and the Cossack Khmelnytsky in 1654.

From about 1950 to 1985, Moscow's policies toward Ukraine varied. Sometimes the government exercised strict control and suppressed all things with a nationalistic theme. At other times, officials were tolerant of writers, allowed the Ukrainian language to be taught in schools, and permitted a revival of Ukrainian culture. The economy continued to be centrally controlled from Moscow, however, with established production quotas and no allowance for laws of supply and demand to work in an open economic market.

The Soviets did attempt to develop Ukraine's industry, especially during the 1950s and 1960s in the eastern Donbas region. During the 1970s and 1980s, however, what had been development suffered greatly from Moscow's bureaucratic mismanagement, and industrial output declined. Consumer goods were of very poor quality and continually in short supply.

Beginning in the mid-1980s, Ukrainian nationalistic themes received renewed, and increasingly open, attention. Premier Mikhail Gorbachev initiated economic reforms (*perestroika*) and more openness of discussion and news dissemination (*glasnost*). Local leaders came forth. The Ukrainian language became the Republic's official tongue. The Greek Catholic church appeared openly from its underground status, and many people returned to this peculiarly Ukrainian faith.

Social movements, such as environmentalism responding to the Chernobyl disaster, emerged, as did labor organizations in the mines and plants of Donbas. Communist delegates to Moscow were defeated at the polls, even when they ran unopposed. A political party, Rukh, came into existence. It advocated democratization and human rights, conditions that were all but nonexistent under Soviet control.

Gorbachev faced increasing nationalistic feelings among the various Soviet republics and tried to institute reforms. This was opposed by hard-line Communists who, in August 1991, tried to oust Gorbachev as head of the Soviet government. The two-day attempted *coup d'etat* (forceful overthrow of an existing government or leader) failed. That same month, the Ukrainian Parliament took advantage of the exploding Soviet political unrest. It declared its independence from the USSR, subject to a popular vote in December of that year. In the election, 84 percent of Ukrainians voted, and 93 percent of them said "Yes" to independence. Ukraine now celebrates its Independence Day as a national holiday each year on August 24.

A capsulized look at the changes in the governance of the city of Lviv over the 20th century illustrates the turbulence that existed in Ukraine during this period. In 1900, Lviv was part of the Austrian Hapsburg Empire. Then Germany controlled it in 1914 at the beginning of World War I. By 1919, it was the seat of the Western Ukrainian Republic, and for a few weeks in 1920 Bolsheviks ran its government. Lviv was part of Poland from 1921 to 1939, when the Soviets gained control. Nazi Germany invaded and held it from 1941 to 1944, when the Soviets once again governed. Finally, in 1991, Lviv became part of an independent Ukraine.

Ukraine has experienced a long, and often tumultuous history. Today, its citizens are self-governing, and they cautiously look ahead to a more stable future. They have set out on the difficult road of transforming Ukraine from borderland to an independent country—a heartland.

Ukrainian-style decorated eggs are a traditional handicraft of the region.

Ukrainians and Their Culture

A description of a people's culture includes the various aspects of their lives—their ways of thinking, doing, and living. How they make their living, how they feed themselves, and how they provide housing are all-important components of culture. So are the ways in which people socially interact and in which a country and its people are governed. Culture also includes their beliefs and how these beliefs and ways of doing things are passed on to their children. Other aspects of culture include architecture, language, religion, heritage, and artistic expression.

Understanding the history of Ukraine helps one to appreciate the mosaic of peoples in the country. History helps to explain their numbers, where they live, their ethnic heritage, language, religion, and other components of their culture. A consideration of the culture of Ukraine and its people begins with population.

Population

In 2000, the population of Ukraine was estimated to be approximately 49,153,000. (The population of the United States in 2000 was approximately 284,500,000.) The country reflects a demographic (the statistical study of the human population) pattern similar to that of many former USSR republics, in which the population has declined since independence in 1991 due to economic and other difficulties.

POPULATION GROWTH RATES (PERCENT)			
	1985–1990	1990–1995	1995–2000
Ukraine	0.37	−1.40	−0.78
United States	0.99	1.07	1.05
World	1.71	1.49	1.35

As of 2001, world population as a whole was growing an estimated 1.3 percent annually, while many former Soviet Republics continued to decline in population.

Because of Ukraine's recent economic problems, couples are discouraged when they think about raising and supporting a family. With an improving economy, the population picture may change. The latest available data, however, anticipate a continuing decline in Ukraine's population. It is estimated that the population will be 43,293,000 in the year 2025, and drop to 37,726,000 by 2050. A declining population can cause problems for a country. For instance, if working-age people move away, then a growing proportion of aging people can strain a country's social security system.

Another indicator of overall human health and environmental health in a country is life expectancy at birth. Currently in Ukraine, overall life expectancy at birth is 68 years; for Ukrainian men, it is 63 years, whereas for women it is 74 years. While world statistics from the 1980s on show a consistent trend of increasing life span, Ukrainian life expectancy has declined during this period, although it appears to be improving now.

LIFE EXPECTANCY AT BIRTH (YEARS)				
	1985–1990	1985–1990	1990–1995	1995–2000
Ukraine	69.1	70.1	67.1	68.1
United States	74.4	75.0	75.6	76.5
World	61.4	63.0	63.9	65.0

An ethnic group is a group of people who share a common sense of history and culture. Most often, ethnicity can be identified by a person's response to the question "What are you?" The ethnic distribution of the population of Ukraine on a national basis includes:

- 72 percent Ukrainians

- 22 percent Russian

- 6 percent others, including Belarussians, Bulgarians, Hungarians, Moldavians, Poles, Romanians, and Tatars in Crimea

In certain parts of the country, this distribution varies. In Crimea, 63 percent of the people are of Russian background, and many Russians also live in the industrial cities of eastern Ukraine.

A country that is divided ethnically often experiences internal conflicts. Each ethnic group wants to exercise its power and desire to control, and those in the minority often feel powerless.

Language

The Ukrainian language is an East Slavic language, as are Russian and Belarussian. The alphabet differs slightly from Russian, but the two languages are mutually intelligible—

that is, readers of one can read and speak the other, at least to a degree. The Ukrainian language is the official language of the country, but it is not the only language spoken by Ukrainians. Russian is widely spoken, especially in the eastern part of the country.

The Slavic languages are part of the Indo-European linguistic family believed to have originated in Persia (now Iran) and spread from there. It was brought to Ukraine with the waves of horsemen that crossed the steppes in early history. The spread westward continued.

The Germanic and Romance languages of Western Europe are derived from the same roots. So, English, French, German, and Italian, among other languages, are related to Ukrainian, because they also are Indo-European languages. The ancient language also spread eastward from its area of origin, and Hindi, spoken in India and elsewhere, is another member of the Indo-European family of languages.

Language has played an important role in Ukrainian history. Conquerors have often forbid the teaching of Ukrainian in schools and its use in official, governmental business. By restricting the use of the language, rulers have tried to eliminate the nationalistic feelings of the people. Their efforts have some basis in fact: a special language can help build a national feeling. During various times in history, Ukrainians revived their language as a way to express their desire for freedom. One of the first measures passed by the Ukrainian legislature on its course to independence from the USSR was to make Ukrainian the official language. In the parts of the country with large Russian populations, however, the Russian language is also widely used.

Religion

Like language, religion can be a unifying element in a country, and a conquering state may suppress it in order to solidify its power.

St. Sophia Cathedral in Kiev was originally built in 1017–1031 A.D. After considerable rebuilding and renovating, it probably retains little of the original structure, but over the centuries it has been a center of religious life in Kiev and has been designated a World Heritage Site by the United Nations.

Ukraine has a unique religion in the Uniate Church, also called the Ukrainian Catholic, or the Greek Catholic church. It came into existence in the late 16th century for historic reasons. Poland and Lithuania, whose people were Roman Catholics, dominated the people of western Ukraine at that time. By agreement, the Ukrainian Orthodox bishops accepted the leadership of the Pope in Rome without giving up their familiar worship and ritual. The Uniate Church, therefore, practices Greek Orthodox forms of worship while acknowledging the Pope in Rome as its leader. At that time, Russian influence in eastern Ukraine was growing, and there was no change to the Orthodox religion of the Cossacks.

In the late 1920s, during a time when Russian dominance of Ukraine was comparatively weak, the people formed an Orthodox church with leadership in Kiev. It was called the Ukrainian Autocephalous Orthodox Church (UAOC). Following World War II, under Stalin and the USSR, the UAOC was outlawed along with the Uniate Church, which had revived after being suppressed by the tsars. The Russian Orthodox Church, with its leaders in Moscow, took over the property of the Uniate Church.

Although the Uniate religion could not be practiced openly after 1948, people continued to practice in secret. In the late 1980s, as Soviet control loosened, the church around Lviv became an open rallying point for Ukrainian activists seeking independence. Because of its history, the Uniate Church has always been strongest in western Ukraine, centered in Lviv. It now has an estimated 4.5 million members. Uniate priests are the only Catholic priests in the world who can get married.

In addition to the Uniate Church, the Ukrainian Orthodox Church (UOC, formerly the Russian Orthodox Church) recognizes the church leadership in Moscow, while the UAOC leaders are in Kiev.

The Roman Catholic Church is strongest in western Ukraine. This reflects the region's heritage of the strongly Roman Catholic Polish and Austro-Hungarian Empires. It has an estimated 1.5 million members.

Religious holidays in Ukraine are celebrated on the Julian calendar, not the Gregorian calendar. The Julian calendar, named for Julius Caesar, who instituted it in the first century A.D., was based on an incorrect calculation of the length of a year. The cumulative effect of this over many years was that months got out of step with the climatic seasons. A new and better calendar, devised by Pope Gregory XIII, came into use in 1582. It adjusted the old calendar by ten days, and should stay correct through many years. Even so, church festivals in the Orthodox faith follow the Julian calendar. So, for instance, Christmas is January 7 instead of December 25.

In Crimea, people of the Tatar community are Muslims. This has historic roots from the 14th century when the Golden Horde adopted Islam. The people of Crimea recognized the supremacy of Ottoman Empire in the late 15th century. The Crimean Tatars trace their ancestry to these peoples.

Historically, Ukraine has had an important Jewish community. At the beginning of World War II, approximately three million Jews lived in Ukraine, equivalent to about 20 percent of the world's Jewish people and 60 percent of Soviet Jewish population. They suffered greatly, however, in the tragic events of the Holocaust. In western Ukraine, only about 2 percent of the Jewish population survived. Today, Ukraine has about 500,000 Jewish people, approximately 1 percent of its population.

The Arts

Ukraine has a long and flourishing artistic tradition. Literature exists from as early as the 10th century. The *Tale of Bygone Years* from the 11th century tells the story of the founding of Kiev by Kyi and his brothers and sister. Through the centuries of suppression, Ukrainian authors and poets have kept alive the dream and aspirations of its people for independence. Taras Shevchenko (1814–1861) is a national hero, a painter, and a writer who suffered for his published work. He was born a serf, but his natural gifts were encouraged as a young man, and he was sent to study painting in St. Petersburg, Russia. His writings helped make the Ukrainian language well regarded for popular and influential literature. Because of his writings denouncing tsarist Russia, he was banished to Siberia for ten years. The tradition of nationalistic writing continued and was an important factor driving the movement for independence.

Another art form with visible heritage in Ukraine is architecture. An early example is St. Sophia Cathedral in Kiev, built from 1017 to 1031. Although its original Byzantine basic design is evident, it has been added to and rebuilt over the centuries, so that little of the original structure remains. Nevertheless, its many domes and side bell towers are a symbol of Kiev, and St. Sophia Cathedral and the related monastic buildings have been recognized with the designation as a World Heritage Site in the United Nations Educational, Scientific, and Cultural Organization (UNESCO) program.

Architectural styles of the many ages are represented in churches throughout Ukraine. In Lviv are Renaissance-style buildings of the 16th century, reflecting the western European influences in that part of the country. The historic center of Lviv is Ukraine's other designated World Heritage Site.

A traditional form of the Ukrainian visual arts is the icon, a small picture painted on wood depicting a religious theme. Icons were painted during and following the 11th century, soon after the Kievan Rus leaders adopted Christianity. Churches and museums display historic pieces.

An icon is a small painting on wood depicting religious themes or figures. Some women brought their icons with them to a Russian Orthodox rally outside the Ukrainian parliament building in Kiev in 1998.

Folk arts and crafts are plentiful. They exist in the hand embroidery work on blouses, belts, table linen, and skirts, and also in ceramic tableware. Parts of the Carpathian Mountain region are known for their carved wooden tools, furniture, and other items. Hand-painted eggs are a tradition that originated in Ukraine, although they are often associated with Russia. The Easter egg, called *pysanka*, traditionally was a dyed egg. Now the eggs may be made of stone, wood, or clay. They are elaborately decorated with paint or dye, often with a coating of wax used to separate color bands in dyeing. They may have simple lines and dots or elaborate geometric designs or floral patterns. The eggs of the different parts of the country may display patterns peculiar to the various regions.

Classical ballet developed in the region, and it later incorporated themes from local culture. Folk dances today often draw on Cossack tradition with movements like the "duck-kick." Classical music, opera, and ballet are performed extensively in Ukraine today.

In summary, Ukrainian culture includes traits that are also displayed in other cultures. It is, perhaps, the special combination of these traits that is distinctively Ukrainian. Conquerors through the centuries have recognized the national importance of the Ukrainian language and the Uniate Church by suppressing them and forbidding their use. Thus, even since independence, the Uniate faith is no longer dominant throughout the country, and in certain parts of Ukraine, the majority of local people do not speak the Ukrainian language.

The influence of neighboring countries is clear in different parts of Ukraine—Poland in the west, Russia in the east, the Muslim community in the south. Since Ukraine was part of the Soviet Union for most of the 20th century, it may be difficult to isolate the new country as totally distinct from its former links. Borscht, the beet-based soup, and Easter eggs, for example, are usually associated with Russia, but they probably originated in Ukraine.

Ukrainians describe themselves as openhearted and welcoming to visitors. Although they have fought for independence at various times in the 20th century, they do not consider themselves militaristic, and as a people, they are peace loving. A set of cultural traits that is peculiar to all Ukraine, and to only Ukraine, is difficult to identify, but a special blend and pattern of traits exists across the county.

On August 22, 2001, Ukrainian lawmakers in Kiev carried the blue and yellow national flag into the parliament building to celebrate the 10th anniversary of Ukraine's independence.

5

The Government of Ukraine

As the USSR's hold was weakening in the late 20th century and change was in the air, the people of Ukraine demonstrated their solidarity one day in 1990: an estimated 500,000 held hands in a human chain that extended along a highway for over 300 miles (483 kilometers)! With the chain, they marked the line where eastern and western Ukrainian republics had united in 1919, demonstrating the peoples' strong desire for a unified country of Ukraine and thus protesting Soviet domination. When the opportunity came to vote their wish for freedom, 84 percent of voters turned out. Not surprisingly, over 90 percent of the voters favored independence in 1991 from the USSR. The new country of Ukraine came into existence with the clear intent of and desire by its people to become a unified state among the world's nations.

Since independence, however, there have been multiple trials and triumphs on the road of nation building—and more can be expected. While the constitution and government structure are *centripetal* (unifying) forces, not surprisingly there is friction. In Crimea, the links with Russia are particularly strong and may act as a *centrifugal* force, pulling Crimea away from the center. The relative strength of the unifying versus divisive elements will have an important influence on the future of the Ukrainians; the desire of ethnic groups to be self-governing can be a very strong force of dissention in a culturally divided land.

Ukraine started independence with secure borders, a position that many nations have lacked historically. Ukraine assumed the borders that had defined it as a republic within the USSR. Their neighbors to the west, Poland, Hungary, and Romania, quickly determined they liked having Ukraine as a protective buffer nation between themselves and Russia. The people of Crimea with Russian heritage have voiced a desire to have Crimea return to Russia. This region had joined Ukraine in 1954, a relatively short time as measured by political history. In the late 1990s, however, by the Treaty of Friendship, Cooperation and Partnership, Russia affirmed the existing borders, in effect renouncing any claim to Crimea.

Structure of Government

Ukraine's administrative structure includes 24 oblasts, or political subdivisions, plus the Autonomous Crimean Republic. This "autonomous republic" designation is based on cultural differences. It recognizes the large Russian population of Crimea, the fact that the Russian language is more widely used than Ukrainian, and the importance of Russian culture and economic links with Russia of this portion of the country.

Ukraine's first president was elected in 1991. Leonid

Kravchuk had been a Communist Party official. Following independence, he adopted the program of Rukh, an organization that had promoted independence and had become a political party. One of his most important decisions was to set a course for economic reform that included a market-driven, rather than a centrally controlled economy.

A constitution was adopted in 1996. The unicameral legislature (consisting of one chamber, or body), or parliament, is called the Supreme Council, or Supreme Rada. Members are elected for a four-year term. It has 450 members (the U.S. House of Representatives has 435 members). The Presidium is a small group of 19 members of the Supreme Council that acts for the Supreme Council between sessions. It also rules on constitutional questions. (In the United States, the Supreme Court does this.)

The executive branch of the government consists of the president, who is the chief of state, the cabinet, and the prime minister, who is the head of government. The president is elected by direct vote of the people for a five-year term and is limited to two terms. The president as of this writing, Leonid Kuchma, was elected to a second five-year term in 1999.

The president nominates the prime minister, who must be confirmed by the parliament. The president also appoints the members of the cabinet who also must be confirmed by the Supreme Council. The prime minister heads the cabinet, and together they manage the administration of the government. The existence of these two positions, president and prime minister, can give rise to controversy. The president can dismiss the prime minister. The president can veto legislation, but a two-thirds vote of the Rada can override a veto.

The Ukrainian Supreme Court is the highest court in the judicial system. The parliament elects its five judges for five-year terms. The Supreme Court administers the country's judicial system.

Until the late 1980s, the only legal political party was the Communist Party. It was banned in 1991, but again became legal in 1993 as one of many parties. Surprisingly, perhaps, in a country that had just gained its independence, the Communist Party was particularly strong. Its leaders, in fact, promoted close connections with Russia, and even advocated dual citizenship.

In 1999, approximately 70 different political parties, many with strong regional interests, had candidates for election to parliament. Because of this, bills proposing reforms are often blocked. Relatively few Ukrainians, however, are registered party members. A change in the distribution of seats in parliament may lead to more influence by effective parties. Each party with over 4 percent of the total vote receives proportional representation in one-half of the seats in parliament. The winning candidates in the various voting districts hold the other half of the seats.

All citizens can vote at age 18. The members of the Communist Party are predominantly older people who oppose reforms, such as privatization of state-owned enterprises. In elections in the late 1990s, the Communist Party gained 25 percent of the vote. The Rukh Party, generally in favor of a market economy and democratic reforms, won 9 percent of the vote. The Socialist Party had over 8 percent. The Green Party, which promotes environmentally friendly policies and is generally neutral on foreign policy issues, received approximately 5.5 percent of the vote.

Military

The president of Ukraine is the Commander-in-Chief of the armed forces. In 1991, at the time of independence, the country had a military force exceeding 700,000. By 1999, however, this number was reduced to about 350,000. Initially,

On March 17, 2002, Ukraine's president Leonid Kuchma (left) and his Russian Federation counterpart Vladimir Putin (right) met with other leaders to discuss broadening economic ties between Ukraine, Russia, and Moldova.

On October 30, 2001, Ukraine destroyed the last of its missile silos in accord with its agreement to give up its nuclear arsenal. This agreement was reached in 1994.

most of the top officers were Soviets; however, most of them were soon replaced and today nearly all of the top military positions are held by Ukrainians.

This is one of Europe's largest armies. It is, however, in need of more modern equipment. Although as a Soviet republic Ukraine had a large nuclear arsenal, in 1994 it agreed to give up its nuclear weapons. They were shipped to Russia to be destroyed. At the same time, the United States and Russia agreed to secure Ukraine's borders should they be threatened.

International Agreements

Ukraine is a member of a number of international organizations. It was a charter member of the United Nations in 1945. When the UN was being organized, Ukraine and what is now Belarus were given seats. Although they were not independent nations, these regions had suffered terribly in World War II. Ukraine was elected to a two-year term on the Security Council in 1999.

Shortly after independence in 1991, Ukraine joined with Russia and Belarus to form the Commonwealth of Independent States (CIS). Since then, eight other former Soviet republics have joined. This group provides a forum for discussion, but it does not have formal authority to act in political and economic matters.

Although Ukraine is not a member of the North Atlantic Treaty Organization (NATO), it cooperates with that organization. It joined NATO's Partnership for Peace program in 1994, and its armed forces have participated in NATO peacekeeping missions in the Balkans.

Ukraine helped form GUUAM (Georgia, Ukraine, Uzbekistan, Azerbaijan, Moldova), an organization of former Soviet republics that are inclined to look toward the Western World for leadership as they work toward building a better future for their countries.

Ukraine's relationship with Russia is important to the people. The economies were totally integrated prior to 1991 with interconnecting roads, railroads and pipelines. In the late 1990s, the two countries signed the Treaty of Friendship, Cooperation, and Partnership. However, despite this pact, several issues have given rise to conflict between the two. One is the presence of a Russian naval fleet that is based on the Black Sea at Sevastopol, the Crimean port. The two countries have agreed that the fleet will remain there, but instead of paying for the use of the port, Russia will forgive some of the money that Ukraine owes for natural gas it receives from Russia.

Ukraine aspires to join the European Union (EU) and has a Partnership and Cooperation Agreement (PCA) in place with that organization. Under the PCA guidelines, however, much groundwork must be accomplished before Ukraine qualifies for full membership.

The United States quickly recognized Ukraine as an independent country and established an embassy in Kiev. America is committed to helping Ukraine during its sometimes difficult transition from a newly independent former Soviet republic to a lively democracy and has provided financial aid. Much of this assistance has been to help build a market economy and to aid people in great need as a result of an economy in transition from centralized control.

The United States also provides assistance in the form of exchange programs, in which U.S. specialists such as business people, individuals who provide technical assistance, and those who help develop civil society participation in democratic institutions work with Ukrainians in these endeavors. Peace Corps volunteers also are in Ukraine. Various academic exchange programs exist, including those that involve college faculty and students from both countries.

A number of United States government agencies also are trying to help Ukraine build solid institutions. Help is being offered to develop a criminal justice system, drug enforcement programs, reliable tax systems, health care delivery, and military training. The United States also is helping to eliminate nuclear arms there and to provide attractive employment in peaceful research for former nuclear weapons scientists.

It would seem that Ukraine embarked on independence with great national unity. The world community welcomed the new country with good wishes and tangible aid.

Institutions of democracy were rather promptly established and, for the most part, they have functioned as intended. The obstacles, however, are formidable; possibly the greatest challenge is in establishing a strong economy.

In April 2002, Ukraine's political landscape assumed a striking new look after voters chose Viktor Yushchenko's pro-Western, pro-capitalist party to lead the next parliament. Yushchenko's margin of victory was slim and the challenges to his plans are colossal. Analysts say that his hopes of transforming Ukraine through tax reforms and by eliminating graft may be undermined by political infighting or may succumb to pressure by the former president who is adverse to such changes.

The stakes are high for Russia and Europe. A key question is whether Ukraine will continue to be mired in corruption scandals or begin to fulfill the promise of becoming a powerhouse on Europe's eastern rim. Regardless of what comes next, Yushchenko's victory is a milestone in Ukraine's post-Soviet history.

The south coast of Crimea has a mild climate similar to that of some areas along the Mediterranean Sea, allowing the cultivation of citrus fruits, flowers, grapes, and other sun-loving crops.

6

How Ukrainians Make a Living

U kraine has most of the things that it needs to develop a strong and diversified economy. It has excellent soils and rich coal and iron resources. It also has an educated population capable of producing a wealth of varied goods and services.

Economies can be measured in many ways. One is the importance of work that different people do. Another is the way wealth and production are controlled and distributed. A country's economic strength is often measured by its total production. This measure, called Gross Domestic Product (GDP), is the value of all goods and services produced by a country in a year. (It does not count the "shadow economy," or items that are not taxed and do not get counted in most government statistics.) As Ukraine develops its market economy, its traditional agricultural segment is of less importance than manufacturing, sales, services, and other businesses.

ECONOMIC SECTORS AS A PERCENT OF GROSS DOMESTIC PRODUCT (GDP)		
	1990	2000
Agriculture	26	14
Industry	44	38
Service	30	48
Total	100	100

Under the Soviet government, all planning was centralized. Each manufacturing facility and mining operation was given quotas (required amounts) for production, and all goods, regardless of quality, were assured a buyer. This is often termed a "command economy," or a "planned economy." Transforming this structure and way of thinking to the "supply and demand" nature of a market-driven economy has been difficult in Ukraine. Immediately after independence and continuing through most of the 1990s, measurements of economic growth declined. Signs of a positive change, however, are now beginning to appear.

AVERAGE ANNUAL GROWTH OF THE ECONOMY (PERCENT)			
	1990–2000	1999	2000
Agriculture	−5.8	−4.2	+5.9
Industry	−11.4	+3.0	+10.9
Service	−11.3	+0.3	+5.5

At the time of this writing, it was estimated that the 2001 gross domestic product would increase approximately 16 percent, with both industrial and agricultural sectors growing about 20 percent.

Sectors of the Economy

Agriculture. Throughout much of its history, Ukraine has relied on its fertile black Chernozem soils as the backbone of its agriculture-based economy. During the Soviet era, Ukraine produced more than one-fourth of the agricultural output of the USSR, including as much as 50 percent of its sugar beet production. It was one of the world's leading "bread baskets." This term, however, may have become outdated during the 1990s. During this period, agricultural activity declined, and it is no longer the most important segment of Ukraine's economy. As the importance of industry, commerce, and services expands, agriculture may never again be the major contributor to the country's economy. But tremendous potential exists for agricultural production to expand and help support an ever-growing world population. Approximately one-third of Ukraine is land under cultivation. The country is the world's largest producer of sugar beets and a major producer of wheat, corn, other grains and cereals, and potatoes. The farmers grow winter wheat, barley, winter rye, buckwheat, and millet. Sunflowers are a crop common in the steppes, raised because the seeds produce valuable cooking oil. The agricultural business also includes food processing and production of cereals, sugar, milk, and other products.

Agricultural products are important exports of Ukraine. Buyers are primarily in Russia and other CIS countries. Export crops include grains, sugar, legumes, dairy products, meat products, vegetables, and oil. Ukraine's trading partners for agricultural products will probably continue to be largely Russia and other former Soviet republics. The European Union, dominated by the countries of Western Europe, is protective of its members' agricultural production and markets and most likely will maintain import taxes and other barriers to Ukrainian agricultural products.

In the drier southern part of the country, crops of tomatoes, peppers, other vegetables, and melons are grown with the help of irrigation. Grapes also are grown for making wines. Throughout the country cattle, sheep, poultry, and pigs are raised. Bees are kept for honey and also because they pollinate various crops. Crimea, with its Mediterranean climate, is especially well suited for orchards and vineyards.

Fishing. Traditionally, fishing has been an important source of food in Ukraine. The Black Sea and the Sea of Azov have yielded large catches, as have several of the major rivers. The fishing industry has declined in recent years, however, because of severe pollution in the country's rivers, lakes, and seas. For example, the Dnieper River has over 60 species of fish, including catfish, perch, pike, chub, carp, sturgeon, and herring, but it is so polluted with human and industrial waste and agricultural runoff that eating its fish is discouraged.

Mining and Industry. Ukraine has a number of mineral deposits, which are basic economic building blocks. Rich coal deposits were discovered in 1721 in eastern Ukraine, in the area of the Donetsky Basin (Donbas). The Donbas region, north and east of the city of Donetsk (Donetske), has been one of the world's most important mining and manufacturing centers since techniques of the Industrial Revolution were introduced in the 1880s.

Hugh iron ore deposits are found in the central part of Ukraine, west of the big bend of the Dnieper River. The city of Krivoy Rog (Kryvy Rih), located at the junction of the Inhulets and the Saksahan rivers, became an important ironworks center in the early 1880s. A railroad linked these iron ore deposits with the coal of Donbas approximately 250 miles distant. Together, Donbas and Krivoy Rog became a booming industrial and manufacturing region. By about 1913, Donbas produced over 85 percent of all Russian coal and over 70 percent of Russian pig iron.

But ironworks eventually gave way to steel mills. A

required ingredient in steel is manganese, and deposits of this mineral are located not far from Krivoy Rog, at Nikopol. It is one of the world's largest deposits of manganese and is most conveniently located near other necessary ingredients for the mills.

And while Donbas's coal deposits initially were readily available near the ground's surface, they have been mined for decades. Most coal reserves now are deep underground, averaging 1,150 to 1,300 feet (350–400 meters) below the surface and coal production has declined in recent years:

1975	221 million tons
1985	199 million tons
1992	139 million tons

In addition to these natural resources, deposits of other mineral ore exist in Ukraine, including titanium, bauxite, and gold. Clay is used in ceramics, pottery, and bricks. A rather unusual mineral deposit found in Ukraine is salt. Crimea has large salt deposits, some up to 600 feet (180 meters) thick in places.

The country's manufacturing plants were severely damaged during World War II. But when they were rebuilt, they were modernized to the level of building and technology at the time of their rebuilding. During the second half of the 20th century, Donbas became one of the world's major industrial production areas for metallurgy and heavy industrial equipment. A chemical industry also was developed, including the manufacture of plastics.

Nearly all of Ukraine's heavy industrial facilities were established during the Soviet period. They were designed to be an integral part of the USSR's nationwide industrial complex. Transportation facilities linked Ukrainian plants and mines with other parts of the USSR. But there were few routes joining Ukraine with its European neighbors to the west. In addition to railroads and electric lines, this is also true of pipelines that carry oil and natural gas. This north-east orientation poses a problem: Ukraine's infrastructure (means of delivery) continues to isolate the country and its economy somewhat from Western Europe.

Energy. In the mid-20th century, Ukraine was a major producer of natural gas, but this has declined. It must now import petroleum products, primarily from Russia. Almost half of its energy comes from the fossil fuels of coal, gas, and oil.

ENERGY SOURCES	
Coal	27
Gas	17
Oil	4
Nuclear	43
Hydroelectric	9
Other	minimal
Total	100

Other Businesses. Some new industries are now being developed in Ukraine. For instance, near Kiev, factories produce cameras, precision tools, clothing, watches, chemicals, and aircraft. Former military production facilities are being converted to make tractors and consumer goods. Donbas manufacturing has developed and changed over time and consumer goods are now made in the area, including refrigerators.

The high-tech industry is a rapidly growing economic sector in Ukraine, one that has developed essentially since independence. Well-known computer product manufacturers active in the market include the American firms IBM, Dell, Apple, Hewlett-Packard, Intel, and Microsoft. Many of these companies have local assembly plants.

Most computer buyers are government offices and

businesses; home use of computers is still quite limited. Software development and manufacture is also a problem. Ukraine does not have strong laws protecting intellectual property rights, which means that people make copies of software without paying full price to the manufacturer and without fear of being prosecuted for theft. A strong law protecting intellectual property rights, with confidence that it will be enforced, would stimulate the legal software industry.

The Economy Since Independence

The economic transition since 1991 has been difficult for the people of Ukraine. Before independence, as part of the centrally controlled economy of the Soviet Union, the government established production targets. In this command economy, markets (buyers) were assured. Products were delivered as instructed, and the recipient had to accept them whether or not they were needed. Factories did not compete with one another. Therefore, there was no incentive to develop and install more efficient production methods or, indeed, to maintain existing equipment. When the USSR disintegrated, there were no longer assured buyers for Ukrainian products. Obsolete and inefficient plants were not competitive in the world market.

Politicians spoke of tying Ukrainian industry to Western markets, but that could not be accomplished overnight. The people who managed plants had traditional ties with Russia. And many of them had personal financial incentives for maintaining their facilities as state-owned. While national leaders saw the need to convert state-owned factories to corporations owned through stock held by individual citizens, they found their policies thwarted by entrenched bureaucrats and plant managers. To modernize Soviet-era factories requires a lot of investment in new machinery, and Ukraine still lacks sufficient investment capital. It also needs considerable time to train new managers. As a result of problems such as these, economic activity declined during the 1990s.

In attempting to reform agricultural production, the government tried to break up the huge collective farms. It wanted individuals to own farms, raise crops, and sell their harvests—and, most important, to keep the money from the sale of their products. The political leaders reasoned that if people were to benefit directly from their own labor, then they would use the most efficient methods and maximize the profits of their work. There were obstacles, however. The former Communists who were in charge of the collectives initially resisted such reforms, because they had a stake in the status quo. And the farm workers had followed central instructions for so long that they were not keen at first on being in charge of their own farms and making decisions. Although privatization of agriculture is happening, the conversion has been slower than initially anticipated.

About ten years after independence, Ukraine abolished the remaining collective farms and forgave past debts that farmers owed the government. The people who worked on each collective received a designated portion of land for their own. They could sell the land, or they could add to it by buying land from neighbors. The workers on some collectives decided to continue to work the land in common. They formed cooperative associations in which they all share the work and the profits. This has resulted in the agricultural economy growing over 20 percent in 2001. The trend now is increasingly toward smaller farms, and it is the privately owned units that are now producing most of Ukraine's vegetables, fruit, meat, eggs, and dairy products.

Converting the coal mining industry to a market system also has been difficult. The mines have been the scenes of many labor strikes, and many of the mines are unprofitable, inefficient, and dangerous. A number of miners have died in accidents. But the mines employ many people and the government subsidizes the operation. That is, the coal cannot be sold for enough money to pay the workers' wages and other expenses, so the government provides the additional funds needed. To close the mines would put a lot of people out of work, and this is politically unacceptable. So the mines continue to operate in a controlled environment. Beginning in about 2000, a few of the unprofitable mines were closed. Some international aid has helped the miners who lost their jobs. Many of them are being trained to find different kinds of employment.

Privatization. One key aspect of encouraging investment in Ukraine is its progress in privatizing firms that were owned by the state during the Soviet period. The Ukrainian government issued "privatization certificates" in the mid-1990s, and by year-end 1996 had distributed them to approximately 85 percent of Ukrainians. The certificates can be exchanged for shares in businesses as the government converts firms to private ownership, thereby privatizing the state-owned enterprises.

By mid-1999, about 45,000 small businesses, such as restaurants and small shops, had converted to private companies. Larger firms were harder to convert, but 7,850 of these (over 70 percent) were in private ownership. When the government no longer controls an industry, then competitive opportunities can open up with other manufacturers or suppliers stepping in to bid for the business.

Ukrtelecom, the Ukrainian Telecommunications Company, is an example. It owns all transmission facilities and administers the wire line infrastructure. It is a huge firm, and there is much debate over whether it should be converted from government to private ownership. Privatization would encourage investment, which is needed to modernize and upgrade facilities. But politicians who fear giving up control of such a large and important industry have resisted this step. Potential growth in the telecommunications business is considered huge with the rapidly growing demand for fax, e-mail, mobile phones, and Internet services.

Businesses such as this small sewing factory have been converted from government controlled operations to private companies since the mid-1990s in a process called "privatization."

After independence, some people were in a position to benefit in inappropriate ways. People in charge of factories, for instance, got government money for the factories, but managed to convert it into personal wealth rather than reinvesting it. Sometimes people, often termed "oligarchs," transferred the money out of Ukraine. This was not helpful at the very time the country needed investment capital and was trying to attract foreign firms to establish businesses. Sometimes the oligarchs turned their businesses into illegal "underground" enterprises, for which they did not apply for required government licenses and pay taxes. Corruption was widespread in the early 1990s, and it continues to create many problems, including making it difficult for Ukraine to regain a reputation for honorable dealing—a trait that legitimate investors insist upon in business activities.

Currency. Shortly after independence, as economic activity declined, the government failed to control the stability of its money (currency). In 1993 there was a time of hyperinflation, in which money rapidly lost its value. One month a unit of currency would buy a loaf of bread; the next month that unit of currency was enough to purchase only a half a loaf. High inflation also wiped out the value of peoples' savings. This was particularly hard on people near the end of their working careers who had saved some money to support their retirement.

In 1996, a new currency was introduced called the "hryvnia" (UAH). It was stable for about two years at US$1 = 2 UAH (a person could buy one U.S. dollar for two hryvnias). But in 1998, the Russian economy suffered a severe decline. Because of the close economic connection between the two countries, Ukraine also experienced a sharp decline in economic activity. In response, the government devalued the currency by about half. At the end of 1999, its value was only US$1 = 5.33 UAH. (A person needed 5.33 hryvnias to buy that one dollar.) This change demonstrates a *decline* in value against the U.S. dollar. In another example, in 1996, 1 UAH would buy 50 cents; in late 1999, 1 UAH would buy approximately only 20 cents. The currency devaluation was a setback to the reforms then underway.

Individual Purchasing Power. One measure of the economic level of a country is the level of its citizens' personal income. Wages of most Ukrainians are low, and the government is notoriously far behind in paying workers in government facilities. As a result, in 1998, 40 percent of Ukrainians were living below the poverty line.

Gross national income (GNI) is the total value of all goods and services produced within a country, including the net income earned by citizens who live abroad. Purchasing power parity (PPP) converts this number to "international" dollars. That is, it takes into account the cost of living in different places and makes it possible to compare income consistently. An "international dollar" in Ukraine has the same relationship to the cost of items in Ukraine as a U.S. dollar has in the United States.

PURCHASING POWER PARITY PER GROSS NATIONAL INCOME			
	1999	2000	Change
Ukraine	$ 3,360	$ 3,710	+10.4%
U.S.	31,910	34,260	+ 7.4%
World	6,870	7,350	+ 7.0%

The PPP table shows how very low the income is of most Ukrainians. It also shows a great year-to-year increase in 2000 compared with 1999. This indicator can be watched in future years to see if a consistent trend shows a continuing improvement in the financial well-being of Ukrainians.

Another indicator might be the number of cars in the country. In 1999 there were approximately 93 cars for each 1,000 people. In comparison, in the United States, there were 760 cars per 1,000 people.

International Links. The United States and other countries, as well as international organizations like the World Bank, are trying to do business with the Ukrainians. Trading ties are being built with countries of Western Europe. U.S. government agencies are prepared to help businesses that want to establish operations in Ukraine. These include Coca-Cola, Pepsi, McDonald's, and some other firms with familiar consumer products. Other firms include large companies in agribusiness, such as Cargill, and in heavy industry, such as John Deere and Boeing.

The World Bank has agreed to lend money to Ukraine on very favorable terms at a low interest rate and with many years before repayment is due. As a condition of the loans, the World Bank requires Ukraine to meet certain benchmarks in developing a market economy. For instance, it must transform some manufacturing plants from state ownership into private corporations. When Ukraine does not meet the benchmarks, the World Bank does not increase the loans. In the ten years beginning in 1991, the World Bank loaned Ukraine $2.2 billion of a total of $2.9 billion that it had agreed to lend when the conditions were met.

U.S. law requires all trading partners to respect U.S. patents, trademarks, and "intellectual property rights." This law is designed to stop the pirating (stealing or illegally reproducing) of U.S. products, such as CDs by popular singers. It means that CDs may not be copied and sold without paying "royalties" to the U.S. companies that produce them. If Ukraine will not pass a strong law protecting intellectual property rights and enforce it, then the U.S. will not allow some Ukrainian products to come into the U.S. to be sold. These are examples of the kinds of complications that can slow economic growth.

Trade continues with Russia, a country with which Ukraine's economy has been tied for many decades. This relationship is encouraged as Ukraine seeks ways to improve the situations of its citizens.

Oil Pipeline. The proposed construction of a pipeline to carry oil from the developing oil fields of the Caspian Sea region to the markets of Western Europe could have a major impact on Ukraine's economy. Several different routes are being considered which go across different countries and have different combinations of pipeline and tanker use. Maritime shipping generally is the cheapest form of long distance transportation for bulky products like oil. A decision on the competing routes must take into account economic, political, and environmental considerations.

Since a country can charge a fee for allowing a pipeline to carry oil across its lands, a pipeline across Ukraine would generate income for the nation's treasury. It would also bring oil to Ukrainian refineries to be processed into gasoline for automobiles and into other petroleum products for its own people. So Ukraine would very much like to have a pipeline crossing the country.

It is helpful to look at a map to see the alternate routes being considered for moving Caspian area oil to Europe. A pipeline could go from the southern shore of the Caspian Sea across Iran to the Persian Gulf and the Arabian Sea and the world's oceans. This may be the least expensive of all the optional routes for a pipeline. The problem with this route, however, is that the U.S. government opposes it for political policy reasons; the supply destined for the United States could be cut off at any time by governments often hostile to U.S. policies.

In another possible route, the oil would go by pipeline from Baku, a city on the west coast of the Caspian Sea, to Novorossiysk in Russia. It would then be loaded onto tanker ships which would cross the Black Sea and pass through the Bosporus Straits at Istanbul into the Mediterranean Sea. The Russians favor this option. One disadvantage, however, is that the pipeline would go through the Chechnya district of Russia, where Russian troops and Chechen people have been fighting for years. The fighting could disrupt the service of

President Leonid Kuchma welded the last joint on the first stretch of a new oil pipeline near Odessa in August 2001. Success in such ventures could be a huge benefit to Ukraine's economy in the future.

the pipeline. Another problem with this route is that the Turkish government objects to additional tanker traffic through the Bosporus Straits; they fear the danger of oil spills and environmental damage.

Another route for Caspian oil to Europe would be by pipeline from Baku through the Republic of Georgia and

Turkey to the town of Jeyhun on the Mediterranean coast of Turkey and then by ship to Europe. This would avoid tankers going through the Bosporus Straits. The pipeline would have to be constructed, however, over difficult terrain in Turkey and would be quite expensive.

Ukraine favors a route from Baku by pipeline through Azerbaijan and Georgia to the coast of the Black Sea at Supsa, Georgia. From there, the oil would go by tanker across the Black Sea to the oil terminals in Odessa and then by pipeline to the town of Brody in northwestern Ukraine, where it would connect with an existing pipeline called Druzhba. The Odessa-Brody pipeline link was completed in 2001. The Druzhba pipeline supplies central Europe. A connecting pipeline of about 186 miles (300 kilometers) could be built to supply this oil to Poland and Germany, thereby enlarging the possible market of users. Although some oil could travel this route now, Ukraine would like to enlarge the facilities to handle a much larger quantity.

Getting oil from the Caspian Sea region into the world market is a huge project. Many corporations and many countries are involved, and pipelines and shipping facilities are enormously expensive. Once the oil starts flowing, however, it can cause a great boost to the national economy. Ukraine has a role in this economic drama that will play out in coming years.

Shadow Economy. This term includes economic activities such as illegal drug dealing and racketeering, and small family enterprises that avoid taxes. The shadow economy that is most troubling, however, is the activity by sizeable firms that cheat and do not pay taxes. In Ukraine, the shadow economy is estimated to account for as much as one-half of the country's total economic activity! This represents a huge amount of money being exchanged outside of the formal, legal framework. The loss is very damaging to the country's economy. It also takes a severe toll on citizens' confidence in their government and on the national psyche itself.

People operate outside of the law for a variety of reasons. In Ukraine, taxes are quite high—as much as 90 percent of profits. Government bureaucrats who administer the laws may have a lot of discretion in how they make decisions, and this may cause bribery to be a way to get something done. Registering a business properly, for example, can be very time-consuming. Many corporate managers simply pay a bribe to speed up the process rather than lose time better spent working on their business.

When people are very disillusioned with the way their government works and when they avoid meeting requirements, then the whole rule of law can break down, with terrible consequences to a society. The government of Ukraine can take action to reduce and eliminate the shadow economy, however. If taxes were lower, people might not mind paying them as much, especially if the government services supported by the taxes became efficient. If officials were better paid, and if the rules were clear and evenly applied, then bribery might disappear. Ultimately this would benefit the entire country, with all businesses being registered and paying taxes. It would also allow the country to collect more accurate data so that it can make more appropriate decisions about its economy.

Corruption. A reality related to the shadow economy is that of bureaucratic corruption. This is most troublesome to foreign companies considering investment in Ukraine, because the country's reputation is that government officials must be bribed before they will respond to a request for service. Organized crime also flourishes in Ukraine. This presence of massive corruption and organized crime discourages many businesses from becoming involved in Ukraine.

Ukraine has rich natural resources, a well-educated populace, and a strategic location. It should be able to develop a thriving economy. Corruption that today stands in the way of achieving this goal simply cannot be allowed to exist.

Soccer is a national pastime and passion in Ukraine, as it is in many countries around the world. This 1999 game in Kiev pitted Ukraine against Bulgaria.

7

Living in Ukraine Today

Today, many Ukrainians are focused on making a living, which can be difficult given the weak economy. The country has a very literate populace, with about 98 percent of its adult population able to read and write. Health indicators have declined in recent years, however, a condition attributed to a shortage of public funds to maintain health clinics. Also occupying the attention of Ukrainians are a number of environmental concerns. The country has a great deal of pollution, including that caused by the nuclear disaster at Chernobyl.

About two-thirds of all Ukrainians live in cities. Regional differences are obvious, both in the urban centers around the country and in the rural communities. Travelers will find many places of interest in Ukraine. And, like many people around the world, Ukrainians are staunch soccer fans!

Education

School begins for Ukrainian children when they are six or seven years old and is required for nine grades. Students can then go to a trade school for vocational or technical training or continue on in high school for another two years. High school graduates are then eligible to attend one of the country's state universities. Beginning in the fifth grade, students take exams each year in each subject. English is a mandatory subject for four to six years beginning in the fifth grade. Private schools do exist and public day-care and kindergarten are available. Ukraine is implementing a 12-year course of study in elementary and secondary schooling. This will be similar to the general educational system in many other countries.

The first institution of higher learning in Ukraine was the Kiev-Mohyla Academy in Kiev, founded in 1615. (The oldest institution of higher learning in the United States is Harvard University, founded in 1636.) Early students learned philosophy and theology, important topics of the times, and the school attracted scholars from many countries. It was much reduced in size and importance, however, by Tsar Peter I in the early 1700s because of its nationalistic teachings. It rebounded later in that century, but became primarily a school for candidates for the clergy in the early 1800s. Since independence, it has been reinstated as a university of general education and is symbolic of the new importance of Ukrainian national spirit.

Ukraine's 98 percent adult literacy rate is quite high among the world's nations. Having almost an entire adult population that is able to read and write is a valuable human resource. Ukraine needs, however, to find a way to retain its people, who often, when able, move abroad in search of better opportunities. During the 1990s, an estimated 500,000 people left Ukraine. Most of these emigrants (people who leave a country) were among its best-educated citizens.

Food

A traveler in Ukraine would encounter a wide variety of local foods. A traditional Ukrainian dish, although often associated with Russia, is *borscht*. This red soup usually includes meat, beans, beets, cabbages, tomatoes, potatoes, carrots, and onions which are simmered together for hours. Borscht is often served topped with sour cream. Another traditional dish, called *varenyky,* is a type of dumpling whose dough is rolled around a stuffing of meat or vegetables and which is then boiled or steamed for a long time.

Sports

Soccer (called "football" in Ukraine) is a national pastime and passion today. It is played in schools (both intra- and intermural), in club leagues, in a popular national league, and internationally. Dynamo-Kyiv is a well-known and highly ranked European team.

Ukrainian athletes enter international competition in a variety of events, and the country can boast of Olympic champions in gymnastics, figure skating, Greco-Roman wrestling, weight lifting, and boxing, among other sports. A gymnast from Kherson, Ukraine, named Larisa Latynina, competing on the Soviet team, won more Olympic medals than any other athlete. Between 1956 and 1964 she won medals in 18 events, including 9 gold medals in 1956. In the 1994 Winter Olympics in Lillehammer, Norway, the figure skater Oksana Baiul won the first gold medal for an independent Ukraine.

Health

Ukraine's environmental and health problems reflect the challenges that face the new nation. Some of the human health problems are caused by environmental pollution.

Respiratory ailments are caused by industrial pollution that sends particles into the air. This is especially bad in the heavily industrialized eastern part of the country near some of the big cities. Also, when water treatment facilities are inadequate, leaving water impure, it can carry bacteria that can cause diseases such as cholera. In 1994 there was a serious outbreak of cholera in Crimea.

The number of people infected with HIV/AIDS in Ukraine is not large in comparison with some countries in the world, but that number is growing rapidly. In 1994, 400 cases were reported. By 2000, the number of cases had risen to an estimated 250,000. (The biggest cause of HIV infection is thought to be drug use injections.)

Chernobyl and Pollution Problems

The place name associated with the world's greatest nuclear disaster, Chernobyl, is in Ukraine, approximately 80 miles (130 kilometers) north of Kiev. The failure of the reactor in 1986 is seared into the national consciousness of Ukrainians. On April 26, one of the reactors at the plant became unstable and exploded. The cause of the disaster was later attributed to human error, poor training and execution, and a faulty design. Approximately eleven tons of radioactive particles were blown into the air. This is many times the radiation emitted when the atomic bomb was dropped on the Japanese city of Hiroshima in 1945.

Immediately after the explosion, no public announcement was made. The wind was blowing toward Belarus and the northwest. Several days later, Swedish scientists detected a sharp rise in atmospheric radiation and sounded an alert. Several days after the explosion, the Soviet government finally acknowledged the danger. By that time, a great many people experienced far greater exposure to radiation than they would have had they been evacuated promptly from the vicinity. About 135,000 people were then evacuated from an area

The failure of the Chernobyl nuclear reactor in 1986 brought Ukraine to the world's attention in a negative light. In the aftermath, clean-up crews encased the plant in concrete to seal off the radioactivity, but it now appears that the casing is breaking up and may be in danger of collapse.

within an 18-mile (30-kilometer) radius of the plant.

The cleanup crews encased the damaged reactor in concrete, but after some years, there was evidence that the "sarcophagus" was deteriorating. Should it become unstable and collapse, it could release a vast dust cloud of radioactive particles. It is estimated that approximately 600,000 people worked in the cleanup effort. The debris and all the vehicles and equipment used in the cleanup have been buried in hundreds of sites in the vicinity.

Thirty-one people died directly as a result of the Chernobyl explosion. The long-term aftermath of this tragic event, however, has affected millions of people. Useful medical records were not kept on people who worked in the cleanup effort, but many workers were exposed to a far higher dose of radiation than is normally considered safe. They dispersed throughout the USSR and cannot now be traced in order to follow their medical histories.

It is estimated that approximately 5,000 people who worked in the cleanup have died of radiation sickness. And an estimated 4.9 million people living in Ukraine, Belarus, and southwestern Russia have been affected in some way by the nuclear pollution (fallout) resulting from the explosion. Over 300 cases of thyroid cancer among children, for example, were reported in the nearby regions the first several years after the accident. This is a very high number for this relatively rare disease.

The 18-mile-radius (30-kilometer-radius) area around Chernobyl that was evacuated after the event remains closed to the public. Today, approximately 15 percent of Ukraine's national budget goes to costs associated with the Chernobyl disaster. This includes pensions supporting the early retirement of the people who worked in the cleanup effort and whose health deteriorated so much that they are unable to work again.

The people who were evacuated were affected in other ways, including experiencing significant psychological stress. The disaster occurred in a farming area; many of the rural people who were evacuated to apartment buildings in cities have found it very difficult to adjust to urban ways and living. Some of them have returned to their homes near Chernobyl and picked up their old lifestyle, even knowing that it is unsafe.

Scientists are studying the reaction of plants and animals to radiation exposure. Both Ukraine and Belarus are considering making the affected area a wildlife sanctuary. Consideration also has been given to storing spent nuclear fuel at Chernobyl. All the reactors at Chernobyl are now shut down. The U.S. has given substantial amounts of aid to help assure that other nuclear power plants in Ukraine are safe.

The long-term contamination is one of the saddest results of the accident. People believe the land will be sick for at least a century. The radioactive contaminants (cesium 137 radioisotope) have seeped into the topsoil. From there, they are picked up by water that feeds into the groundwater, which is the source of moisture for plants and animals. That chain then leads to the people who eat them. The silt that is washed into the rivers is radioactive and is carried downstream. Sediment with radioactive particles is accumulating behind the dam on the Dnieper River located downstream of Chernobyl and just north of Kiev. The full extent of this pollution is not known. Kiev's Chernobyl Museum interprets this tragic event with photographs of cleanup crews at work and the repercussions of the nuclear disaster.

The Chernobyl accident helped give rise to an environmental movement in Ukraine. (A strong reaction against the Soviet government because of the accident also strengthened the independence movement.) The ecological movement attracted scientists, journalists, and environmental activists from all across Ukraine. Since independence, a political party with an environmental agenda, the Green Party, has developed. Although small, it does have representatives in parliament and keeps government officials alert to environmental issues.

Beyond Chernobyl

Ukraine has severe environmental problems in addition to the contamination from Chernobyl. With all its economic suffering for the first ten years after independence, Ukraine has had little money to devote to environmental issues other than Chernobyl. One huge legacy of Soviet industrial and military policy is some of the world's most polluted areas. Discharge from smokestacks in industrial areas cause respiratory problems. Cars typically burn leaded gas, and in cities this pollution is particularly pronounced. The runoff of pesticides and fertilizer from agricultural fields is detrimental to water quality of the rivers; it causes unnatural algae growth, which reduces dissolved oxygen in water so that fish, and the organisms they feed on, cannot survive. Sewage treatment plants often are inadequate, and the discharge of human waste from cities flows to the major rivers.

Historically, the Black Sea was a source of a vibrant fishing industry yielding dolphin, mackerel, anchovy, and sturgeon (producing caviar). The catch has declined dramatically, with a parallel loss in jobs and revenues. The pollution has also been detrimental to the tourist business on the Black Sea coastal towns and beaches. To reverse the trend of growing pollution in the Black Sea, many countries, including Ukraine, will have to work together.

Many Ukrainians worry about poor environmental quality, but there still exists the need to develop a widespread environmental consciousness. People raised under the Soviet mind-set may not be aware of the environmentally damaging consequences of industrial activity. Laws that penalize polluters need to be enforced. In some places, environmental subjects are appearing in school curricula and university training. Some environmental nongovernment organizations (NGOs) are forming. The World Wide Fund for Nature (WWF) participates in a consortium of NGOs and others focused on the Danube River and in Ukraine on the Danube delta.

Traveling the Regions

Many developing countries have a major city that dominates urban life, often several times as large than the next largest city. This can cause difficult problems in providing adequate housing, transportation, and utilities for the people who come to this one "prime" city looking for jobs. Ukraine does not have an urban problem of this nature. Kiev, although a large city, does not dominate the country's urban centers. Five cities have populations greater than one million, and these cities are located in different parts of the country. They are Kiev, Kharkiv in the northeastern part of the country, Dnepropetrovsk centrally located at the big bend of the Dniester River, Donetsk in the industrial east, and Odessa in the south.

A traveler in Ukraine would notice regional differences that reflect both the different historic experiences and landscapes of the country. With two-thirds of Ukrainians living in cities, the major urban centers are a focus of the country's various regions. A traveler could see the range of cities and landscapes by beginning in Kiev and making a loop to the southwest to Lviv, then to the south to Odessa and Crimea, then to the eastern manufacturing centers, and finally to the northern forests and lowlands.

Kiev. The capital and largest city is a major focal point of Ukrainian life today. Kiev is the center of government and has important industrial and scientific research institutions. It also houses major cultural and sporting events. The land around Kiev is relatively flat and forested under natural conditions. The city itself has much natural parkland. New factories must locate outside the city beyond a greenbelt district.

Kiev has many sites and monuments associated with Ukrainian history. As already mentioned, the domes of St. Sophia Cathedral are a defining symbol of the city. The Podil section of Kiev, located along the riverbank below the bluff where the main part of town lies, is the historic commercial area from the earliest times.

The Caves Monastery, about two miles (three kilometers) south of the heart of Kiev, also dates to the Kievan Rus period.

Kiev is the capital and largest city in Ukraine. Many important government and educational institutions are located there, including the prestigious Kiev University.

The complex includes several churches, other buildings, and underground caves where the monks lived. Mummified bodies of monks line the passageways in the caves. In addition to going into the caves there, visitors can also see beautiful gold jewelry crafted by Greeks of Scythian times and found in burial mounds nearby.

Outside Kiev is a site associated with World War II atrocities and the Holocaust. In 1941 the Nazis ordered Jewish people of the city to assemble for transfer away from their homes. In fact, they were taken only a short distance to Babyn

Yar and killed. About 34,000 people died in that massacre. Over the course of the next two years, thousands more died in the concentration camp there.

Lviv. Lviv is the major center in western Ukraine. A Galatian prince founded it as a fort on a hilltop in the mid-13th century. The site was selected as a fortification among the mountain passes of the Carpathians. From the ancient castle site, one has a 360-degree view of the city and environs. The architecture and other features of Lviv and western Ukraine reflect the long time the area spent as part of Poland.

The region near Lviv has forests, rivers, and lakes. The Dniester River originates in this area and flows to the Black Sea. Carpathian National Park is in the mountains not far from Lviv, and Ukrainians often hike and ski there in season. Forestry is an important industry, helping Lviv to become an important furniture-manufacturing center.

South of Lviv is the city of Ivano-Frankivsk, located in the northeastern foothills of the Carpathian Mountains. The region has natural resources of oil and gas, gold, and manganese. About 40 miles (65 kilometers) south of Lviv is Kolomyya, founded in the 13th century on the salt trade route between Galicia and the Black Sea. The town of Kolomyya is known as the cultural center of the Hutzuls culture, ethnic Ukrainians of the Carpathian Mountains. They are known for their traditional crafts of carved wooden tools, boxes, and furniture, as well as embroidered folk dresses. This is also the area of the Carpathian Biosphere Reserve, which protects Europe's last virgin beech forest.

In the far western reaches of Ukraine is the city of Uzhhorod, which has existed since at least 903. It is near the Ukrainian borders with Slovakia and Hungary and not far from Romania, and many people in the city trace their heritage to these countries. This region, known as Transcarpathia, has deposits of iron and copper. Farmers raise cattle and sheep and the agricultural products of grapes, vegetables, and winter grains. Tourism is important to the area's economy, including winter ski resorts located in the mountains. Ukrainians calculate the center of Europe as being a point in these mountains near the town of Rakhov.

Odessa. The city of Odessa is a major port and is also known for its appealing beaches. Catherine the Great of Russia had the city rebuilt in the late 18th century after her forces conquered the area. It sits on a high promontory. One of its distinctive features is a broad stairway, called the Potemkin Steps, that leads to the shore of the sea from the heart of the town. With 12 flights of 20 steps each, it is an impressive approach to the Black Sea.

The opera house in Odessa is considered one of the most beautiful in Europe. In addition to being a cultural center, the city has several important academic institutions and film studios.

Odessa's economy has fared better than many since independence. Privatization has proceeded more rapidly and people enjoy a higher standard of living than many of their countrymen. Machine building is an important industry, as is oil refining. The city is also a resort center. People come to "take the waters" at several waterfront spas and to apply the local mud, which is said to have curative properties. The region is known also for its sparkling wine, that is made from local grapes.

Kherson is a city located at the mouth of the Dnieper River, on the Black Sea between Odessa and Crimea. It has an important shipbuilding industry. Traveling from Odessa to Crimea, one passes near the Askeniya Nova Reserve. It covers an area of about 13,350 acres (33,000 hectares), and preserves steppe grassland that has never been plowed.

Crimea. On the Crimean Peninsula, Simperopol is the regional capital city and is located in the interior. Sevastopol is the naval port that was the target of siege in the Crimean War and is now the base of the Russian fleet. But the coastal city of

The Potemkin Steps are a famous landmark in the seaside city of Odessa. They form a dramatic connection between the harbor and the town center. The steps are named for the cruiser *Potemkin* whose crew mutinied in 1905 rather than fire on strikers on shore.

Yalta may be Crimea's best known community. Near Yalta is the Nikitsky Botanical Garden that houses plants from almost every country in the world. Started in 1812, it has some 28,000 species of plants, including 200 species of roses.

The beaches along the Crimean coast attract vacationers from Ukraine and Russia. Tsar Alexander II built a lavish summer home in Livadia, several miles from Yalta. This is the exact location of the 1945 Yalta Conference attended by Stalin, Churchill, and Roosevelt, at which they decided the fate of parts of Europe at the end of World War II.

Other Russians built more modest vacation homes, called *dachas,* along the coast. Tolstoy vacationed here, as did Chekhov, and it was in Crimea that he wrote two of his best-known plays, *The Cherry Orchard* and *Three Sisters.*

The mountains of Crimea that block the cold northern winds help give the narrow coast strip its mild Mediterranean climate. They contain olive, cypress, and cork oak trees. Many of the rocks that make up the basic geology of Crimea are of limestone, which often fosters the formation of caves. The Kara-Dah Nature Reserve protects some of the unusual rock formations of the region.

The Eastern Region. A large city in the northeast is Kharkov, which is a regional center of culture. It was founded in the mid-17th century by Cossacks and is now a manufacturing center with factories making tractors, engines, and mining equipment. The factory that previously made T80 tanks now makes equipment for coal mining and sugar refining. The Antonov aircraft factory is here.

The town of Donetsk, with a population of over one million, is a major regional center. It has a university, an array of shops, and is a cultural center with theaters and a philharmonic hall. The area around Krivoy Rog is known for the manufacture of mining machinery, diamond drills, cement, foodstuffs, and timber. The city has a school to train miners and a teacher education center.

Between Kharkov and Kiev is Poltava, the site of the 1709 battle in which the Russian tsar, Peter the Great, defeated the Cossacks and their allies, ending their bid to form an independent Cossack state.

The Northern Region. North of Kiev, the grasslands give way to forested land and then, approaching the border with

Belarus, to marshlands and wetlands. Chernobyl is in this area, and foreign visitors are comparatively rare. The northwestern region, the Rivne district, is forested. Its mineral resources include basalt and stones for construction materials. The highest elevation in this administrative district, far from the Black Sea, is only 341 feet.

The Chernitov region northeast of Kiev used to be an agricultural area. Its forests were prime sites for gathering mushrooms and wild berries. It is no longer safe to eat these local delicacies. The people now are quite poor, although they continue to raise cattle, pigs, and tobacco.

Following this route through the regions of Ukraine enables a traveler to see and experience the full variety of Ukrainian landscapes, cultural centers, economic activities, and historic influences. It reveals the diversity of a people who seek now to build the country's future as a single nation.

Kiev has been a center of Slavic civilization for centuries and has importance as the "mother city" for a huge region that is now divided into many countries. This Friendship Arch was built to commemorate the 325th anniversary of the reunion of Russia and Ukraine.

8

Outlook for the Future

U krainians demonstrated their sense of unity visibly in 1990 with their human chain made up of a half-million people joining hands. As they translate this feeling into patriotism for a new nation, the success of three spheres appears to be pivotal: the government, the economy, and the environment.

Since independence, Ukraine has accomplished a great deal toward establishing its presence in the society of nations. For instance, Ukrainians have written and adopted a democratic constitution and held elections within its framework. The government has negotiated several important treaties. The country's boundaries with Russia were secured with the Treaty of Friendship, Cooperation, and Partnership, and they have reached agreement with Russia on the use of the naval base at Odessa for the Russian fleet. They have turned over to Russia Soviet nuclear arms that were in the country, and have signed the nuclear nonproliferation treaty.

In spite of the country's great need for power, it has closed the nuclear plant at Chernobyl, shutting down the three remaining reactors that remained in operation after the disaster in 1986.

Ukraine has worked with NATO peacekeeping efforts, and has begun discussions with the European Union on the distant goal of membership. The country also has expressed interest in joining the World Trade Organization. Ukrainians have hosted visits from leaders of the United States, including President Clinton in 1995 and 2000, signifying cooperation and good will (and delivery of some much needed foreign aid funds). Ukraine has cooperated with Russia on launching satellites into space and has a continuing program of Antarctic research.

Since gaining its independence, however, the Ukrainians have experienced considerable hardship. Yet economic indicators from 1999 to 2001 have shown an improving trend. Much of the economic growth and development depends on Ukraine having a dependable legal framework. The country has a high literacy rate and a technically trained workforce, both of which are vital to economic success. A strong and enforced law protecting intellectual property rights must be put in place. This would give foreign firms confidence their rights would be honored. It would also be a step toward admission to the World Trade Organization and toward opening wide the doors of the global economy to Ukraine.

The country's shadow economy, representing possibly as much as half of all its economic activity, is a huge drain on the national treasury, since the goods and services changing hands are not taxed. The shadow economy is also a deterrent to foreign investment. If not checked, failing to comply with legal requirements will become a way of life. The activities of organized crime must be curbed as well; the term "Mafia capitalism" must cease to be relevant to Ukraine.

It is difficult for the government to monitor activities and take appropriate actions when so much economic activity operates outside of legal channels. Another problem is the great swings of boom and bust cycles that make the country more vulnerable to external influences. In the mid-1990s, when Russia experienced an economic downturn, the Ukrainian economy suffered severe shocks. Ukraine must develop an economy that is not so fragile. The means of achieving this goal are now in hand. They include privatization, foreign investment, and establishing links with the global economy through the WTO and regional economic groups.

Businesspeople in the United States look toward Ukraine as a market for products and as a trading partner. Opportunities exist in several areas. Agricultural machinery is in demand in Ukraine and could be made there by foreign investors. (Transporting this heavy equipment can be expensive.) Equipment also is needed to improve airline service and air traffic control systems. As the country's construction business grows, there is a demand for building materials and equipment. Pharmaceuticals and equipment in the medical and dental fields are also needed. Energy companies and power systems need equipment and parts, such as motors, pumps, transformers, fans, turbines, and meters.

The telecommunications business is in need of modernization, giving rise to demand for fiber optic lines. Demand for modern communications can be expected to increase dramatically. Ukrainian businesses and individuals want extensive and reliable telephone service, as well as e-mail and Internet access, and fax and mobile phone lines.

The potential for increased tourism also offers many opportunities for investment. Kiev and other major Ukrainian cities are large cosmopolitan centers, but they lack hotels with the amenities and services that most Western business travelers desire. The historic architecture and sights, as well as the recreational opportunities of Ukraine's natural landscapes, would attract tourists as well.

U.S. firms considering investing in the Ukrainian market could approach it in several ways. They could build plants to manufacture or assemble parts locally. They could form a joint venture with a Ukrainian partner. They could send a sales representative to sell their products and take orders, and then ship the items directly to the customer from a U.S. plant.

Each of these and other possible arrangements has special considerations and consequences. U.S. and Ukrainian license and customs fees vary. The cost of investment, taxes, and duties must be considered, as must possible limits on bringing profits back home to the United States.

As Ukraine pursues economic development, the accompanying social and environmental concerns must be addressed. If agricultural and industrial output is increased at the cost of further pollution of the waterways and air, then it will be a costly trade-off. Developing renewable energy sources would reduce dependence on fossil fuels and could greatly benefit the air quality. Upgrading municipal wastewater treatment plants would reduce the human waste that flows into the rivers. Careful application of agricultural chemicals would reduce the toxic runoff from fields that flow into the waterways.

Some projects would require great investment, such as care for the land around Chernobyl and the people harmed by the explosion, its cleanup, and the continuing exposure to radioactive particles. Some environmental issues require cooperation with neighboring countries. And Ukraine's own people must be educated about the many benefits of protecting the environment from harm.

People of differing backgrounds across the country can be expected to continue to press for recognition and special rights. For example, the Tatars were harshly treated in their expulsion from Crimea by the Soviets. As they return, they expect particular help as they reestablish their homes. Also, their demands for either independence or incorporation as a part of Russia have not been realized.

Because of its longstanding links with Russia, Crimea has special standing in Ukraine as an autonomous republic. Eastern Ukraine as well has economic links with Russia and a strong Russian influence as evidenced by their dominant use of the Russian language. But the political influence of this region's people who seek economic integration with Russia should decline as Ukraine's economy strengthens and trade ties are established with other nations.

Features of Ukraine's physical landscape—the steppe grasslands, the many large rivers, the rich soil, and the wealth of natural resources—have helped shape the its people and their history. The periods of formal nationhood have been comparatively rare and short-lived in recent centuries, but a new opportunity came with independence in 1991. The Ukrainians will shape their future with their own resolve and the support of other countries, both neighbors and more distant states. They face a great challenge of building a modern, market-driven economy. This must be pursued while they work to reduce causes of pollution and clean up past environmental damage. But this is not the first time in their history that the people of Ukraine have met challenges. In looking to the future, they can draw on many proud traditions and proven strengths.

Facts at a Glance

Land

Geographic Coordinates	Kiev: 50° 27′ North, 30° 30′ East
Total Area	233,090 square miles (603,700 square kilometers)
Comparative Size	About 99% the size of Arizona and New Mexico combined
Climate	Primarily midlatitude temperate continental. Mediterranean climate on south coast of Crimea. Summers warm generally; hot in south. Winters cool on coast; cold inland. Precipitation highest in north and west; less in east and southeast.
Terrain	Primarily level, gently rolling steppe. Carpathian Mountains in southwestern area. Crimean Mountains in southern Crimea.
Elevation Extremes	Lowest point: Sea level (0 feet [0 meters]) at Black Sea Highest point: Mount Hoverla, 6,762 feet (2,061 meters)
Natural Resources	Arable land, coal, iron ore, manganese, titanium, bauxite, salt, timber, natural gas, oil
Land Use	Arable land: 58% Permanent crops: 2% Permanent pastures: 13% Forests and woodland: 18% Other: 9%
Natural Hazards	Earthquakes in Crimea
Environment–Current Issues	Radioactive contamination from Chernobyl nuclear disaster in 1986; acid rain and industrial pollution of air and waterways; coastal pollution; deforestation

People

Population	48,760,000 (mid-2001 estimate)
Age	0–14 years: 17.3% (male 4,310,000; female 4,128,000) 15–64 years: 68.6% (male 15,965,000; female 17,468,000) 65 years and older: 14.1% (male 2,275,000; female 4,615,000)
Population Growth Rate	– 0.78%
Ethnic Groups	Ukrainian 73%, Russian 22%, other 5%
Religions	Orthodox, Uniate (Ukrainian Catholic), Protestant, Jewish
Languages	Ukrainian, Russian, Romanian, Polish, Hungarian
Literacy	(Defined as people age 15 and older who read and write) 98%

Facts at a Glance

Government

Dependency Status	Independent
Government Type	Republic
Capital	Kiev
Administrative Divisions	24 oblasts, 1 autonomous republic (Crimea)
Eligibility to Vote	All citizens 18 years of age or older
Executive Branch	President is chief of state, elected by popular vote. Prime minister is head of government, appointed by president, approved by Supreme Council. Cabinet of ministers appointed by president, approved by Supreme Council.
Legislative Branch	Unicameral Supreme Council, or Rada (450 seats).
Judicial Branch	Supreme Court, Constitutional Court

Economy

Gross Domestic Product (GDP)	$189.4 billion (2000 estimate)
GDP Growth Rate	16% in 2001 (estimated)
Purchasing Power Parity per Gross National Income	$3,710 in 2000 (increase of 10.4% over 1999)
GDP—by Sector (2000)	Agriculture: 14% Industry: 38% Services: 48%
Inflation Rate	25.8% (2000)
Industries	Coal, electric power, ferrous and nonferrous metals, machinery and transport equipment, chemicals, food processing
Agricultural Products	Grain, sugar beets, sunflower seeds, vegetables, beef, milk
Exports (value)	$14.6 billion (2000 estimate)
Exports—Commodities	Ferrous and nonferrous metals, fuel and petroleum products, machinery and transport equipment, food products
Exports—Partners	Russia 24%, Europe 30%, U.S. 5% (2000 estimate)
Imports (value)	$15 billion (2000 estimate)
Imports—Commodities	Energy, machinery and parts, transportation equipment, chemicals
Imports—Partners	Russia 42%, Europe 29%, U.S. 3%
Currency	Hryvnia (UAH)
National Holiday	Independence Day, August 24 (1991)

History at a Glance

700–400 B.C.	Scythian civilization flourishes.
500–600 A.D.	Slavic peoples migrate into Ukraine.
5th century	Kiev founded, according to legend and archeological evidence. Kyi, two brothers and sister, establish Kiev on Dnieper River.
882	Oleg wins control of Kiev, marking the beginning of Kievan Rus period.
988	Valdimir (Vlodymyr) the Great adopts Christianity for himself and the people of Kievan Rus.
1017–1031	St. Sophia Cathedral is constructed in Kiev.
1240	Batu Khan leads Mongols in the conquest of Kiev.
1569	Lithuania and Poland unite, and Kiev comes under Polish rule.
1596	Most Ukrainian Orthodox bishops accept Catholicism, and Greek Catholic church begins. Union of Brest.
1615	Kiev-Mohyla Akademy, founded; first Ukrainian institution of higher learning.
1648	Cossack hetman Khmelnytsky defeats Poland at Battle of Pyliavtsi.
1654	Khmelnytsky pledges loyalty to Russian tsar in exchange for military aid.
1667	Treaty of Ardrusovo formally partitions Ukraine between Poland and Muscovy (Russia), roughly along the Dnieper River.
1709	Russia defeats Cossacks and their allies at Battle of Poltava.
1772–1795	Partitioning of Poland, whereby much of western Ukraine is transferred to Russia.
1775	Russian army of Catherine the Great destroys remaining Cossacks.
1783	Russia annexes Crimea.
1854	Crimean War breaks out between Russia on one side and Ottoman Empire, Great Britain, and France on the other. Florence Nightingale nurses British soldiers in Crimea.
1856	Treaty of Paris marks end of Crimean War.
1918	Ukrainian National Republic founded.
1921	Treaty of Riga signed, providing for transfer of parts of western Ukraine to Poland, Romania, Czechoslovakia, and the majority of land to Russia.
1922	Ukrainian Soviet Socialist Republic is incorporated into the Union of Soviet Socialist Republics (USSR).

1932–1933	Ukrainians suffer devastating famine resulting from the policies of Joseph Stalin.
1939	Molotov-Ribbentrop pact between Russia and Germany signed, providing for mutual nonaggression and noninterference with internal politics and military.
1939	Soviet Red Army advances into Polish Ukraine.
1941	German army attacks Russian Ukraine.
1941–1944	Nazi Germany occupies Ukraine.
1944	Stalin forces Tatars to leave their homes in Crimea.
1945	Franklin D. Roosevelt, Winston Churchill, and Joseph Stalin meet in Yalta and decide how Allies will administer European countries after World War II.
1945	Ukraine joins United Nations as a charter (original) member.
1954	Soviet premier Khrushchev transfers Crimea to Ukraine in commemorating 300th anniversary of Russian–Ukrainian union.
1986	Reactor at Chernobyl nuclear power plant explodes.
1989	Rukh independence movement founded.
1986–89	Soviet premier Gorbachev establishes *perestroika* and *glasnost*.
1991	August: Ukrainian parliament declares independence from USSR.
1991	December: Ukrainians vote overwhelmingly for independence.
1994	Ukraine, Russia, and United States sign agreement calling for Ukrainian nuclear disarmament.
1994	Leonid Kuchma elected president of Ukraine.
1996	New currency, hryvnia, introduced.
1997	Treaty of Friendship signed by Russia and Ukraine (ratified in 1999). Russia renounces claims on Crimea. Ukraine agrees that Russian fleet can remain at Sevastopol for 20 years.
1998	Ukrainian Communist Party wins approximately one-fourth of seats in Rada.
1998	Currency (hryvnia), devalued by 51 percent.
1999	Kuchma elected to second five-year term.
2000	Chernobyl nuclear power plant shut down.
2002	In parliamentary elections, party of the president won 23%; opposition party of Viktor Yushchenko won 25%; Communist Party won 15%.

Glossary

alluvium: Collection of silt, clay, similar material carried by a flowing river and deposited as sediment.

Bolsheviks: Violent Russian revolutionaries, responsible for overthrowing Russian tsar in 1917 and establishing Communist Party.

borscht: Ukrainian soup made with beets, other vegetables, meat; often topped with sour cream.

Chernozem: A rich, fertile soil found in much of Ukrainian steppe grasslands; a type of mollisol.

CIS: Commonwealth of Independent States; organization of 11 former Soviet republics.

dacha: Country retreat.

glasnost: Political openness. Policy instituted in mid-1980s by Soviet premier Gorbachev.

hetman: Cossack chieftain, leader. Elected.

Hetmanate: Government under a hetman.

hryvnia: Unit of Ukrainian currency.

Khazars: People of empire based at mouth of Volga River; traders with Kievan Rus in eighth and ninth centuries.

mollisol: A type of soil, rich in organic matter and important for agriculture.

oblast: Regional administrative unit, comparable to a state or province.

oligarch: One of very few people who are politically or economically powerful.

pysanka: Ukrainian Easter egg.

perestroika: Restructuring; refers primarily to Soviet economic policy of late 1980s characterized by less central control of industry and agriculture.

Rada: Ukrainian parliament; also called Supreme Council.

Rukh: People's Front of Ukraine for Reconstruction, founded in 1989; became a movement for independence. After 1991, a political party.

Scythian: Civilization in Ukraine, c. 700 B.C.– 400 B.C.

Slav: Ethnic peoples, originally from Central Asia, who migrated to Russia, Eastern Europe, Ukraine.

serf: Peasant who worked the land under the control of the landowner; essentially a slave.

steppe: Vast area of level or gently rolling land, typically naturally covered in grasses.

Tatars: Mongols, Muslims who settled in Crimea.

Trypillian: Early documented culture in Ukraine, about 4000 B.C.– 2000 B.C.

tsar: Title of Russian rulers before 1917.

Uniate Church: Christian faith utilizing Orthodox forms of worship while acknowledging leadership of Roman Catholic Pope.

Varangians: A branch of Vikings from Scandinavia who established Kievan Rus society in Ukraine in 9th century; also known as Rus.

NAMES

Traditional Spelling	Ukrainian Spelling
Chernobyl	Chornobyl
Dnepropetrovsk	Dnipropetrovsk
Dnieper River	Dnipro River
Dniester River	Dnister River
Donets'k	Donetske
Kharkov	Kharkiv
Kiev	Kyiv
Krivoy Rog	Kryvy Rih
Odessa	Odesa

Further Reading

Berkmoes, Peter Ver, et al. *Russia, Ukraine and Belarus.* Oakland, CA: Lonely Planet Publications, 2000.

Toll, Nelly S. *Behind the Secret Window: A Memoir of a Hidden Childhood During World War II.* New York: Dial Books, 1993. Author recalls her experiences when she and her mother were hidden from the Nazis by a Gentile couple in Lwów, Poland during World War II.

Ukrainian Embassy. Online at *www.ukremb.com/ukraine.*

United States Central Intelligence Agency. *CIA—The World Factbook, Ukraine.* Online at *www.cia.gov/cia/publications/factbook/geos/up.html.*

United States Department of State. *www.state.gov/r/pa/bgn/3211.htm.* May 2000.

For more information on Ukraine and Ukrainians go online at *www.brama.com.*

Agriculture, 10, 11-13, 17, 20, 22, 24-25, 29, 30, 40-41, 69-70, 71-72, 76, 93, 94, 97-98, 101, 105, 106
Ancient history, 29-30
Animal life, 27
Architecture, 9, 33, 54, 95, 97, 105
Ardrusovo, Treaty of, 37
Area, 9, 16
Arts, 53-54, 56-57
Askaniya Nova Reserve, 26-27, 98
Autonomous republic, 60, 107
Azov, Sea of, 19, 27, 72

Babyn Yar, 96-97
Batu Khan, 33
Beaches, 13, 94, 98, 99-100
Bees, 17, 72
Biosphere Reserves, 26-27
Black Sea, 9, 13, 15, 17, 19-21, 29, 32, 72, 94, 97, 98
Borders, 9, 10, 15, 16, 19, 21, 43, 60, 103
Britain, 37-38

Cabinet, 61
Capital city. *See* Kiev
Carpathian Biosphere Reserve, 27, 97
Carpathian Mountains, 19, 21, 22, 32, 56, 97
Caspian Sea, and oil pipeline, 82-84
Caves Monastery (Kiev), 95-96
Chemical industry, 73
Chernitov region, 101
Chernobyl, 101
   and nuclear disaster, 11, 44, 87, 90-93, 104, 106
Cholera, 90
Churchill, Winston, 43, 100
Cities, 21, 23, 37, 38, 43, 72, 87, 95-100, 105
   See also Kiev
Climate, 20-21, 22-23, 72, 100
Coal, 25-26, 38, 69, 72, 73, 76-77
Collective farms, 41, 76
Commonwealth of Independent States (CIS), 65, 71

Communist Party, 62
Computers, 74-75
Constitution, 60, 61, 103
Consumer goods, 44, 74
Corruption, 67, 79, 84-85
Cossacks, 10, 36-37, 44, 52, 56, 100
Crimea, 19, 23, 35, 37, 43, 49, 53, 60, 72, 73, 90, 95, 98-100, 106-107
Crimean Mountains, 21-22, 27
Crimean War, 37-38, 98
Culture, 9-10, 16-17, 19, 29, 30-31, 33, 41, 44, 47-50, 52-54, 56-57, 60, 95, 97, 98, 100
Currency, 79-80
Cyrillic writing style, 13, 33
Czechoslovakia, 40, 43

Dairy products, 11, 71, 76
Dams, 19, 93
Dnepropetrovsk, 95
Dnieper River, 17, 19, 21, 30, 32, 33, 37, 72, 93, 98
Dniester River, 19, 97
Donbas region, 38, 44, 45, 72, 73, 74
Donets Basin, 25-26
Donetsk, 95, 100

Economy, 9-12, 19, 40-41, 43, 44, 48, 60, 61, 62, 67, 69-77, 79-85, 93-94, 97-98, 100, 104-106, 107
   See also Agriculture; Mineral resources
Education, 39, 41, 69, 87, 88-89, 100, 104
Elections, 60-61, 62, 67, 103
Energy resources, 11, 19, 74, 82, 87, 97, 106
   See also Nuclear power plants
Environmental issues, 11-12, 20, 44, 62, 72, 87, 89-94, 101, 106, 107
Ethnic groups, 49, 60
European Union (EU), 66, 71, 104
Executive branch, 61

Fishing industry, 20, 72, 94
Folk arts and crafts, 56, 97

Index

Foods, 11, 56, 71, 72, 89, 93
Foreign investment, 104, 105-106
Foreign policy, 60, 62, 65-67, 71, 79, 93, 103-104
Forests, 13, 17, 27, 29, 95, 97, 100, 101
Friendship, Cooperation, and Partnership, Treaty of, 60, 65, 103
Furniture manufacturing, 97
Future, 45, 60, 103-107

Galicia, 32, 35, 39-40, 41, 43, 97
Germany, 41-43, 45, 96-97
Glasnost, 44-45
Gorbachev, Mikhail, 44, 45
Government, 10-11, 45, 59-62, 64-67, 84-85, 95, 103
Grains, 24, 25, 30, 71, 98
Greeks, 9, 30, 32, 96
Green Party, 62, 93
Gross Domestic Product (GDP), 69, 70
GUUAM, 65

Hapsburg Empire, 37, 45
Health care, 11, 48-49, 87, 89-90
High-tech industry, 74-75, 77
History, 9-10, 13, 16-17, 19, 27, 29-45, 47, 50, 52, 95, 107
Hitler, Adolf, 41
HIV/AIDS, 90
Holocaust, 42, 43, 53, 96-97
Honey, 17, 72
Hoverla, Mount, 21
Hryvnia (hv), 79-80
Huns, 30

Icons, 54
Independence Day, 45
Independence movements, 10, 13, 40, 43-44, 50, 54, 57, 107
    and Soviet Union, 10-12, 13, 15, 16, 45, 50, 56, 59-60, 62, 66-67, 70, 75-77, 79, 93, 103, 107
Industry, 11-12, 26, 38, 44, 70, 71, 72-73, 74, 75, 90, 95, 97, 98, 100, 105-106
Intellectual property rights, 75, 81, 104

International agreements, 60, 65-67, 71, 103-104, 105
Iron, 25, 26, 38, 69, 72
Islam, 35, 53, 56
Itil, 31, 32
Ivano-Frankivsk, 97

Jews, 31, 36, 42, 43, 53, 96-97
Judicial system, 61-62
Julian calendar, 53

Kharkov, 95, 100
Khazars, 31, 32
Kherson, 98
Khmelnytsky, Bohdan, 36-37, 44
Khrushchev, Nikita, 44
Kiev, 16, 19, 22, 23, 30, 32-33, 36, 38, 40, 42, 43, 52, 53-54, 66, 74, 88, 95-97, 105
Kievan Rus, 32-33, 35, 54, 95
Kolomyya, 97
Kravchuk, Leonid, 60-61
Krivoy Rog, 26, 72, 100
Kuchma, Leonid, 61

Languages, 9, 13, 30, 33, 35, 44, 49-50, 54, 56, 60
Legislature, 61, 62, 67
Life expectancy, 48-49
Literature, 39, 41, 44, 53-54
Lithuania, 9, 10, 35, 37, 52
Livestock, 30, 41, 72, 76, 97, 101
Location, 9, 15-16
Lviv, 37, 45, 52, 54, 95, 97

Manganese, 73, 97
Metallurgy, 72-73
Military, 62, 64, 74
Mineral resources, 10, 25-26, 38, 69, 72-73, 76-77, 97, 101
Mongols (Golden Horde), 33-35, 53
Mountains, 17, 21-22, 27, 56, 97, 98, 100

Nationalism, 38-40, 40
National parks, 26-27

NATO, 65, 104
Natural gas, 26, 74, 97
Natural landscape, 10, 16-17, 19-22, 107
Natural reserves, 26-27
Natural resources, 10, 11-13, 17, 24-26, 27, 38, 69, 71, 72-73, 76-77, 93, 97, 101, 107
Nightingale, Florence, 38
Nikopol, 73
Nuclear power plants, 104
    and Chernobyl disaster, 11, 44, 87, 90-93, 104, 106
Nuclear weapons, 64, 66

Oblasts, 60
Odessa, 21, 37, 38, 95, 98, 103
Oil, 26, 74, 82-84, 97, 98
Oleg, 32
Oligarchs, 79
Orchards, 72
Orthodox Christianity, 33, 35, 41
Ostrogoths, 30
Ottoman Turks, 9, 19, 35, 37-38, 53

Perestroika, 44-45
Pereyaslav agreement, 37
Podil section (Kiev), 95
Poland, 9, 10, 35, 36-37, 40, 41, 43, 45, 52, 53, 56, 97
Political parties, 45, 61, 62, 67, 93
Poltava, 100
Population, 10, 48-49
Ports, 98
Potemkin Steps (Odessa), 98
Power plants, 11, 19
    See also Nuclear power plants
Prairies, 13, 17, 24-25
Precipitation, 22-23
President, 60-61, 62, 67
Presidium, 61
Prime minister, 61
Pripet Marshes, 21
Privatization, 76, 77, 79, 81, 98, 105
Purchasing power parity, 80

Railways, 26
Rakhov, 98
Recreation, 13, 22, 87, 89, 94, 95, 97, 98, 99-100, 105
Religion, 31, 33, 35-36, 39, 44, 50, 52-53, 54, 56
Rivers, 17, 19, 21, 30, 31, 32, 97, 106, 107
Rivne district, 101
Roman Catholicism, 35, 53, 54
Romania, 40
Roosevelt, Franklin, 43, 100
Rukh Party, 45, 61, 62
Russia, 9, 15
    and Crimea, 60
    naval fleet of, 65-66
    and nuclear weapons, 64, 103-104
    and oil pipeline, 82
    and relationship with Ukraine, 60, 64, 65-66, 67, 71, 79, 103-104
    and Tatars, 106
Russian Empire, 10, 54
    and Cossacks, 36, 37, 52
    and Crimea, 37-38
    and partition of Ukraine, 37
    and Revolution, 40
    and Ukrainian culture, 56-57
    and Ukrainian nationalism, 38-39
Russian language, 50, 60
Russian Orthodox Church, 52

St. Sophia Cathedral, 33, 54, 95
Salt deposits, 73
Scandinavians, 9, 31-32
Scythians, 10, 30, 96
Serfdom, 36, 37, 38
Sevastopol, 22, 38, 65, 98
Shadow economy, 84-85, 104-105
Shevchenko, Taras, 54
Shipbuilding industry, 98
Simperopol, 23, 98
Slavs, 30, 31
Soccer, 87, 89
Socialist Party, 62
Soils, 10, 11-13, 17, 24-25, 69, 71, 93, 107

Soviet Union, 10-12, 17
  and Chernobyl disaster, 90, 93
  and pollution, 94
  and Russian Revolution, 40
  and Tatars, 106
  Ukraine part of, 11, 40-45, 52, 56,
    62, 64, 70, 71, 73-74, 75, 77, 94
  Ukrainian independence from,
    10-12, 13, 15, 16, 45, 50, 56, 59-
    60, 62, 66-67, 70, 93, 103, 107
  and World War II, 41-43
Sports, 87, 89, 95
Stalin, Joseph, 41, 43, 44, 52, 100
Steel mills, 72-73
Steppes, 13, 16-17, 22, 24-25, 27, 29,
  30, 36, 37, 71, 98, 107
Sugar beets, 71
Sunflowers, 71
Supreme Council/Rada, 61, 62, 67
Supreme Court, 61-62
Sviatoslav, 32

Tale of Bygone Years, The, 53-54
Tatars, 35, 36, 43, 53, 106
Taxes, 85
Telecommunications, 77, 105
Tennyson, Alfred, Lord, 38
Time zone, 16
Tourism, 94, 98, 105
Trade, 30, 32, 33, 71, 74, 81, 104
Transcarpathia, 97
Trypillians, 29-30

Ukraine, meaning of, 10
Ukrainian Autocephalous Orthodox
  Church (UAOC), 52
Ukrainian language, 13, 33, 44, 49-50,
  54, 56
Ukrainian Orthodox Church, 52, 53

Ukrtelecom, 77
Uniate Church, 35-36, 39, 44, 52, 56
United Nations, 65
United States
  and direct investment, 74, 81,
    105-106
  and nuclear power plants, 93
  and nuclear weapons, 64, 66
  and oil pipeline, 82
  and relationship with Ukraine, 64,
    66, 81, 93, 104, 105-106
Uranium, 26
Uzhhorod, 97-99

Valdimir the Great, 32-33
Varangians, 31-32, 32
Vegetables, 71, 72, 76, 97
Vegetation, 13, 17, 25, 101
Vikings, 17, 31-32
Vineyards, 72, 97, 98
Volga River, 31
Volhynia, 32, 35
Voting rights, 62

Water features, 17, 19-21, 27, 32, 97, 106
Water supply, 11, 90, 93, 106
Wetlands, 21, 27, 101
Winds, 20, 22, 100
World Bank, 81
World Trade Organization, 104, 105
World War I, 11, 40-41, 45
World War II, 11, 41-43, 53, 65, 73,
  96-97, 100
Writing style, 13, 33

Yalta, 22, 99-100
  Conference at, 43, 100
Yushchenko, Viktor, 67

About the Author

CATHERINE W. COOPER earned a Master of Arts degree in Geography at the George Washington University, where she is a Research Fellow with the Institute for Urban Environmental Research. Cathy is also a member of the adjunct faculty of the Geography Department.

CHARLES F. "FRITZ" GRITZNER is Distinguished Professor of Geography at South Dakota State University. He is now in his fifth decade of college teaching and research. Much of his career work has focused on geographic education. Fritz has served as both president and executive director of the National Council for Geographic Education and has received the Council's George J. Miller Award for Distinguished Service.